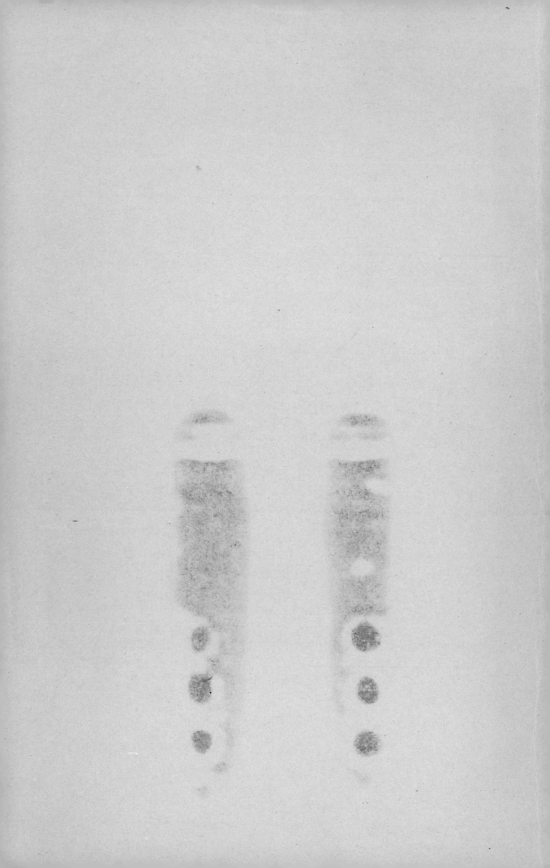

GOLDEN GATE

THE PARK OF A THOUSAND VISTAS

Viaduct Bridge on Main Drive

Golden Gate,

THE PARK OF A THOUSAND VISTAS

By

KATHERINE WILSON

WITH ILLUSTRATIONS BY THE AUTHOR

THE CAXTON PRINTERS, LTD.
CALDWELL, IDAHO
1947

Printed, lithographed, and bound in the United States of America by
The CAXTON PRINTERS, Ltd.
Caldwell, Idaho
62218

FOREWORD

The story of Golden Gate Park is in a singular sense the story of a city's growth in character—of the evolution of its spirit, of its appreciation of cultural and ethical values, of its innate talents and capacities. Because this park is pure creation, conceived and wrought out of crude materials into a thing of beauty, it is an expression of all these and so, as is any work of art, a physical presentment of the spirit of its creator. Since it is also unique of its kind in the world, it is in that sense, too, identical with the city that made it. As an interpretation of it, this volume is offered in tribute to the soul of a great city.

ACKNOWLEDGMENTS

For the material in this book I am indebted to the following sources: Reports of the San Francisco Park Commission; Reports of the De Young Museum; Papers from the Academy of Sciences; *The Pacific Coast Metropolis* by John P. Young; *San Francisco, a Pageant* by Charles Caldwell Dobie; *"Northern California Writers' Project, W.P.A.";* the *San Francisco Chronicle; The Magic Park* by Robert Barbour Johnson; and to the generous assistance of many individuals, notably Superintendent Julius Girod, Eric Walther, Dr. Robert C. Miller, Miss Sidney Stein, Miss Alice Eastwood, Cary M. Baldwin, Robert Owen, Lewis C. Allen, Frank Slattery, Peter Rock, and George P. Moran, each of whom has contributed valuable data and personal reminiscences to the chronicle. To all these I extend my appreciative thanks.

THE AUTHOR

CONTENTS

		PAGE
1.	THE PARK—ITS LURE AND HOW IT CAME TO BE	13
2.	ITS PRESIDING GENIUS—JOHN McLAREN	25
3.	ITS PATTERN	39

Roads and Trails
The Water System
The Lakes
The Meadows

| 4. | THE CONCOURSE . . . . | 51 |

De Young Memorial Museum
California Academy of Sciences
The Steinhart Aquarium
The Temple of Music
The Oriental Tea Garden

| 5. | THE PARK FLORA . . . . | 75 |

The Strybing Arboretum and Botanical Garden
The Conservatory
The Park Nursery

| 6. | ANIMAL LIFE IN THE PARK . . . . . | 93 |
| 7. | NATURAL MEMORIALS . . . . | 101 |

John McLaren Rhododendron Dell
Redwood Memorial Grove
Heroes' Grove
Historic Trees
Liberty Tree
Hoover Tree
George Washington Bicentennial Grove
De Laveaga Dell
Shakespeare Garden of Flowers
Huntington Falls
Marx Meadow

PAGE

8. OBJECTS OF HISTORIC INTEREST . . . 109
   Prayer Book Cross
   The *Gjoa*
   Pioneer Log Cabin

9. RECREATION GROUNDS 115
   Kezar Stadium
   Golden Gate Park Stadium
   "Big Rec"
   Children's Playground
   Miscellaneous Sport Grounds

10. REMEMBRANCE OF THINGS PAST . . . 125

SUPPLEMENT 137
   Monuments and Memorials
   Recreational Activities
   Map of the Park

8

ILLUSTRATIONS

Viaduct Bridge on Main Drive . . . . . . Frontispiece

FACING PAGE

Entrance — Eighth Avenue 14

Junipero Serra 39

Dutch Windmill 42

An Island—Stow Lake 43

Lindley Meadow 46

De Young Museum from Fourteenth Avenue 56

Across the Concourse: Temple of Music and De Young
    Museum 68

Entrance to Tea Garden 69

Tree Ferns 76

The Conservatory 85

Buffalo Meadow 93

Pioneer Log Cabin 110

Carousel—Children's Playground 116

Portals of the Past 125

Oriental Urn 134

9

THE PARK

ITS LURE AND HOW IT CAME TO BE

*T*HE Rhododendrons Are Blooming in Golden Gate Park!" With this lyric paean, placarded in early May on city streetcars and motor buses, proclaimed by boxed displays in city plazas, and reported as news in the daily papers, blossom-loving San Franciscans are yearly notified of the spring floral spectacle awaiting them in that arboreal theater which is San Francisco's particular pride and delight. It is the signal for a city-wide, bay-wide pilgrimage to the largest man-made pleasance in the world, the go sign for a gathering throng of sightseers, itself almost rivaling in kaleidoscopic color that of the gorgeous masses of bloom on every hand. Then do the Park driveways flow with cars, the grassy meadows become dotted with picnicking groups, the bridle paths and leafy trails threaded by equestrians and strolling couples; all come to view a pageant of natural beauty unsurpassed anywhere in the world, and all, perhaps, gone just a bit fey with the enchantment of it.

But splendid as is the springtime, with its rainbow-banks of rhododendron and azalea, camellia and acacia, the snowdrift of its tea plant, the saffron of its genista, the olive- and bronze- and russet-green of its burgeoning new leafage—bewilderingly lovely as is

13

the early year, no season can claim solely for its own the beauty of Golden Gate Park. For this thousand acres of greensward and woodland has been so designed as to accord to every quarter of the year its full share in the fiesta of color and fragrance that goes to make this one of the most famous garden spots of the world. From May through January to May again, the Park is the happy hunting ground of those who seek, and find there, the beauties of all the seasons.

If there is no other city that takes to its soul quite the same degree of unction in the possession of a thing distinctly its own as does San Francisco with its unique Park, it may be for the reason that there is no satisfaction comparable to that which comes of creative achievement. And Golden Gate Park is in the most literal sense pure creation, a thing wrought by human hands without benefit of nature, out of nothing more substantial than a dream and a faith, on a foundation no more constant than wind-blown sands. Other cities have their spacious parks, but parks on sites already given something of a hand by nature—sites offered by fertile meadows or wooded slopes, watered by natural springs or streams, and more or less tempered to ravaging winds, or at least within reasonable access to these advantages. Not so San Francisco! When she came to select a setting for a city park, whether from sheer perversity or a serene confidence in her own genius, she chose the most unprepossessing terrain imaginable—miles from the city center a great

Entrance—Eighth Avenue

expanse of shifting sand dunes rolling back from the ocean beach, the only water in sight that of the salt Pacific breaking on its shores, its only vegetation a few willows and scrub oaks, gnarled and dwarfed under incessant bludgeoning by trade winds out of the west. Such was the spot which today, cutting a great green swath through a sector of the metropolis, is a thousand-acre tract of giant trees and massed shrubbery, acres of floral bloom, miles of charming vistas, grassy meadows, paved driveways, bridle paths and foot trails, the scene of a score of mirroring lakes and cascading waterfalls, of deer runs and buffalo paddocks, a wildfowl refuge—a great playground for old and young. It is, besides, the setting for a great museum and art gallery; of aquatic, botanical, and natural history museums; an outdoor music concourse and temple; a tropical conservatory, an arboretum, two athletic stadia, tennis courts, ball fields, and miscellaneous game places—the whole a remarkable educational recreation ground for the millions of the city and its neighboring communities. Such is Golden Gate Park, its claim to world-wide fame resting upon the fact that, the largest of its kind in the world, it is a thing artificially made into something supremely natural. Obviously, San Francisco has more than a common right to her pride in it!

It must be confessed, however, that the plan for a great city park such as this did not spring full panoplied from the minds of San Franciscans. The first

California settlers, Spaniards from Mexico, were used to a treeless landscape. To them there was nothing incongruous or unsatisfying in the barrenness of the hills rolling back from San Francisco Bay. They were quite content with such plant life as their women could coax into being by aid of watering pots within their adobe-walled patios and such food crops as the padres were able to raise around the missions. Little more concerned with growing things were the American settlers that came on the Spaniards' heels, who found in a climate averaging sixty degrees of temperature in summer no special call for shade. Even today San Franciscans out of doors invariably seek, not the shady, but the sunny, side of the street. It was not until the city began to regard itself with an eye to permanence, with some awakening to the gracious arts of living, and found a spur in recent examples of park creations presented by New York and Philadelphia, that the citizenry recalled the elm-shaded streets, the maple- and chestnut-dappled groves of their native states and began to consider the advantages of a city park for San Francisco.

A few forward-looking citizens actively supported the idea. But when it came to looking about for a suitable site it was to discover, with some dismay, that the best lands in or contiguous to the city had already been appropriated. In 1868 Mayor Frank McCoppin, the motive force behind most of the progressive movements of that day, ordered the board of supervisors to make a survey of sites available for a system of city parks. The board recommended certain areas in that section of the city west of Divisadero Street toward the beach, and with these a strip of land not less than two hundred feet east of high-water mark along the entire ocean front for boulevard purposes.

And immediately controversy arose. There had long been dispute over ownership of lands in this section, which had been parts of the pueblo of San Francisco, ceded to the government under the old Spanish and Mexican land grants. To some four square leagues of this land the city of San Francisco claimed title, though it was an area of little more than sand dunes cluttered with huts and shacks, the evidences of the squatters' rights under which it was being held by certain individuals who refused to surrender their holdings. A decision in favor of the city's claim had been handed down in 1864 by Judge Field, of the circuit court, the decree having been entered in May, 1865, and subsequently approved by an act of Congress, thus, apparently, ending the long dispute. But these "squatters" happened to be prominent and influential citizens whose power in both the common council and the state legislature was sufficient to block any moves the city might make to take possession. It was simpler to "proposition" than to fight them. Therefore, in 1868 Mayor McCoppin appointed a committee of citizens to make an appraisal of such lands as were desired for park purposes. This com-

17

mittee consisted of Dr. R. B. Cole, C. H. Stanyan, A. J. Moulder, Monroe Ashbury, and Charles Clayton. In spite of the discouraging nature of the land, the committee valued the portion desired for public use at just under $1,300,000. It was found that an assessment of 10¾ per cent on the whole would produce enough to pay for the land wanted at 90 per cent of its appraised value. At this figure the squatters capitulated and the park site was purchased for $810,-595. In 1870 the legislature created, and Governor Haight approved, the first five-man Park Commission for supervision of the property, and the board was organized in May of that year. For the record, the members of that first commission were: S. F. Butterworth, president; D. W. Connelly, C. F. McDermott, A. J. Moulder, secretary; Abraham Seligman, treasurer; and William Hammond Hall, surveyor. Patrick Owen was named park keeper. From the appointment of the commission until the adoption of the new city charter in 1900, the Park commissioners were appointed and their acts controlled by the state. After that the commissioners were appointed by the city's mayors and their jurisdiction was over all the city's parks.

Thus, finally, the Park project was under way, but not before it had become a butt of ridicule and worse in the community. To make a park out of a thousand acres of barren land, to expect to grow trees and grass on hills of sand forever adrift before driving winds—

18

it was a crazy idea! Jokes and jibes and caustic criticism of San Francisco's "Park" were a favorite indoor sport for many a day.

And it would, in fact, have been the height of folly to attempt to grow in this wasteland the kinds of trees familiar to the settlers from the New England states and the South. Elm, chestnut, birch, live oak—these were poor stuff for the grim battle for existence that faced any growth here. But farther down the coast, near Monterey, were the rugged cypress and pine that had rooted among the rocks and sands, and clung there in the face of every assault by the elements. And there was a blue gum from Australia, called eucalyptus, that the Spaniards had found to be quick-growing and stubborn before both wind and drought. Then, in spite of everything, the tract itself was not without its merits. It was not all sand. Here and there among the billowing hills were outcroppings of rock, and there were long, wide swales and sinuous valleys, all of which held intriguing possibilities to the imagination of a landscape gardener. And in the countryside about were other hills of rock and clay, sources of material for surfacing roads and trails.

So, while the townfolk jeered, the gardeners went to work. The grounds were surveyed and the landscape plan designed by William Hammond Hall, under whose direction also were laid out the principal driveways of a system which has been followed, with but few changes, to the present day. To the insistence of

19

Hall must be credited the wideness of the driveways as well as the serpentine pattern of the roads, this to break the force of the winds. And it was Hall who undertook the first control of the sand. At the extreme eastern end of the tract, at what is now the "Panhandle," in the lee of some hillocks, were growing a few scrub oaks and willows. Here a start was made. Small boys were hired to go out into the hills and collect seed from the wild lupine and this, together with beach grass and, later, bent imported from European coasts, was sown to provide anchorage. Wherever a plant took root, making any sort of shelter, there were then tucked seedlings of cypress and pine and gum, germinated in the Park Nursery built for the purpose. Thousands of these seedlings were nested in the sand. Gradually, as the young trees grew and took courage, they began to conspire against the elements. In huddled groups they made sheltered spots for less sturdy growths. Soon around them appeared leaf and bud and blossom. In that first year acres and acres of grass and twenty-one thousand trees were planted, while four miles of macadam roads were made. Later, Kentucky bluegrass was sown in the meadows, while on the hillsides madroñas, manzanitas, and laurel were made to take hold. Meanwhile, thousands of tons of soil were being hauled from near-by hills and mixed with the sand to give it ballast. To cover an acre of land one foot in depth, sixteen hundred cubic yards of loam are necessary. To sustain trees of ordinary size

20

there must be at least a three-foot depth of nourishing soil. It is easy to estimate the quantities of material that had to be brought to build the soil for even this first small area of the Park. Humus and peat, straw, grass cuttings, and tons of manure were spaded into it. Street sweepings from the city, hauled to the Park site in dump cars, also went into its making—material that for years had been finding its way to "Butcher Town" and the mud flats, or had been hauled down the peninsula for vegetable gardens.

Thus, little by little, fertile soil was made, and little by little the tawny dunes took on tints of green. Grass and shrub and tree grew where none had grown before. And at last there came a day when San Franciscans, looking out to sea across the onetime reaches of rolling sand, found themselves gazing upon hundreds of acres of verdant park land, lush and inviting in the morning sun.

ITS PRESIDING GENIUS
JOHN MCLAREN

*U*NTIL 1887 the Park was under the direction of a succession of superintendents. Then John McEwen, who in 1882 had followed William Hammond Hall (resigned to become state engineer), appointed as his assistant a young man named John McLaren, a landscape gardener employed on an estate in San Mateo County. In 1890 when McEwen resigned, McLaren succeeded him. And from then until his death in 1943, John McLaren was the Park's presiding genius.

So inseparably has the name of John McLaren come to be identified with Golden Gate Park that to mention the one inevitably brings reference to the other, and in the minds of many Californians, and others, is the erroneous idea that the Park itself owes its existence to the labors of this one man. But to say that Golden Gate Park had been flourishing for twenty years before John McLaren took it over is not in any sense to detract from the value of the service rendered by one whose peculiar genius was for over half a century devoted with supreme consecration to its development, and whose persistence in the pursuit of his own high standards of beauty and usefulness brought it to its present consummation.

Young McLaren had long had an eager eye on those sandy wastes near the metropolis where this experiment in park making was going on. He was a Scot, born at Sterling on December 20, 1846, of a heritage characteristically revealed in an anecdote he used to tell of his father who, chiding him for idleness, took him aside one day and said: "Me boy, if ye've naething to do, go plant a tree an' it'll grow while ye sleep." That in the course of his life John McLaren planted more than two million trees would indicate that his father's advice sank in. At any rate, he took up gardening, studying at the Edinburgh Botanical Gardens —he is said to have been the only student of Edinburgh University to graduate merely as "Gardener"—and he came away with the conception of gardening as a fine art that remained the inspiration and stimulus of his entire life. He arrived in America and California in the late sixties while San Francisco was still in the braw stage of its own youth, but had already taken steps to create a park on the city's sand dunes. His own experiments in San Mateo had convinced him that plants and trees could be grown in sand if one took the trouble to sow the kind of grass that would anchor it, and he hankered to have a hand in what was being undertaken at Golden Gate Park. It is ironic now to recall that his appointment as superintendent, at the instigation of William Hammond Hall, who had continued in an advisory capacity on the Park board, was strongly opposed in certain influential quarters on the ground that he lacked the proper qualifications for the job! But neither then nor through the years that followed did John McLaren let shortsightedness or powerful influence interfere with what he had set out to do, and he took over the work of developing Golden Gate Park with that stubborn determination and energy which over the years became familiar to many a citizen who had the temerity to oppose him in the pursuit of his ideals. Yet, toward the end of his life, when, the recipient of many degrees and honors from colleges and horticultural societies, he was hailed throughout the world for his work in the creation of one of its unique beauty spots, it was not so much this of which he was proud as of his triumph over a tough and stubborn obstacle. For then and always he referred to himself, not as the Park's creator, but only as "the boss gardener who conquered the sand."

With his appointment as superintendent of the Park, McLaren was authorized to visit some of the famous parks of England, Scotland, and France, where he studied plans and methods and made personal associations that proved valuable in later years. At once, too, he began writing letters to park superintendents, horticulturists, and nurserymen all over the world, asking for specimens of flowers, trees, and shrubs. Little by little, as his purpose became known, his requests were answered, and donations began coming in. There were seeds and roots and cuttings from such widely different quarters as New Zealand, South

America, China, Japan, Spain, Italy, the Alps, Greece, Syria, Algeria, Ceylon, and Madagascar, the West Indies, Scotland, Bermuda, England, Hawaii, and Java. John McLaren is recognized as the greatest introducer of exotics (nonnative plants) that the West has known. Meanwhile, experiments were being carried on in the Nursery and out of doors in the Park with plants and seedlings native to North America, and particularly those adapted to the climatic conditions of California. In the old Nursery thousands and thousands of seedlings were germinated, and cuttings and roots made ready for planting outdoors.

For those interested in statistics it is recorded in the "Reports of the Park Commission" that in 1889-90 there were planted 167,364 trees and shrubs, 874 vines and trailing plants, 480,000 herbaceous and flowering plants; while in the Nursery, awaiting transplanting out of doors, were more than 205,000 other trees and shrubs, 9,051 deciduous plants, and 3,921 aloes, palms, and grasses. In the Park at that time there were already some 500 varieties of trees and shrubs, and 253 varieties of herbaceous and flowering plants. In the Conservatory were a hundred varieties of tropical plants, thirty-nine varieties of palms, fifty-four of orchids, seventy-three of ferns, and seventy-one of various other types of growth. With the years, of course, this collection has been steadily and enormously augmented, and today there is no park in the world where so great a variety of trees, shrubs, and plants from all parts of the earth have been so successfully cultivated. It is said that of the trees of the Temperate Zone only the beech and sugar maple have refused acclimatization in the Park.

In the development of Golden Gate Park John McLaren had but one aim, though this was twofold: to create a recreation ground for beauty and utility. Beauty—in contours, in vistas, in groupings and harmonious associations of texture, color, and form—this was his first objective in planning. Utility—the creation of a place where, in the inspiration of this beauty, the people could gather freely and without irksome restrictions for their pleasure and health and growth into good citizens—this was his second aim. To these ends he devoted every waking moment of his life. He followed one principle—and one only: always to work with nature, never against her; never to interfere with the beauty the Creator had given us. And on this principle he bent all his efforts toward building a landscape of natural charm. The formal, the artificial, the unnatural, he abominated. In all his planning he followed nature's lead, utilizing such shapes and contours and outcroppings, such rises and depressions, as he found at hand, for such plantings as were happiest and most at home in those settings. Out of this policy came the massed loveliness of shrubbery and seasonal bloom that lines the driveways, the long, grassy meadows and shaded dells, the charming vistas, the invitingly winding roads and pathways, the flower-

29

banked lakes, the rollicking cascades, the groupings of trees, and the towering groves that are the never-ending and enchanting surprises of Golden Gate Park. Out of it, too, came the great grassy meadows and slopes, the secluded nooks, where every day in the year thousands of the city's old and young come to loiter in the sunshine, at picnic gatherings or in gossiping groups on the benches, or prone on the ground in pursuit of a rugged sun tan. In Golden Gate Park there have never been any "Keep Off the Grass" signs to interfere with this salamander instinct. Every inch of the Park where growth is secure is accessible to the people. All of which is highly eloquent of the humanity of the man that made it so. For Uncle John was very jealous of his plants. Shrubs and trees were a passion with him; they were his children. He guarded them with his life. Someone has said of him: "He was a ferocious man when anything threatened his Park. Better one's right arm wither than that it should stretch forth a hand to break one of his trees." Yet precious as these were to him, he gave of them freely so long as the gift was not abused.

As superintendent of the Park his life was a constant battle against the forces of ugliness and artificiality—too often in the guise of progress. Once, when it was proposed to run a trolley line through the Park, Uncle John emitted a roar that was heard the length and breadth of the city. Though the promoters assured him that they would not disturb any planting that might be in the way, the Scotsman took no chances. The night before the line was to be laid he rounded up his army of gardeners and set them to work. They worked all night, and in the morning everywhere across the proposed right of way were discovered growing trees and shrubs and beds of flowers. The trolley, happily, was never built.

Almost to the end of his life he fought the "stookies" —stookies being the statues of this and that and the other famous figure with which hero-worshippers have sought to punctuate the Park. The advent of each new stookie sent Uncle John off into a new frenzy of planting, to screen as much as possible of the artificial bronze or marble replica with natural growth. In his lifetime only one of these was left unshrouded in greenery. This was the statue of Bobby Burns, whose poetry the Scotsman never wearied of reciting. He was horrified when a stookie of himself was introduced into the Park, and he saw to it that it occupied a space as inconspicuous as could be found.

It would be absurd to expect a man of such pronounced and stubborn ideas to survive through more than fifty years as the guiding hand of a great city project and escape criticism and opposition. More than one attempt was made to oust him. But what John McLaren was doing for the people of San Francisco was something the people understood. And the "Old Man" was widely beloved. City administrations came and went, but John McLaren stayed on. Writes

31

Charles Caldwell Dobie, in his *San Francisco, a Pageant*: "Grafting mayors, reform mayors, timorous mayors, corporation mayors, labor union mayors, fiddling mayors and mayors who sell flowers—not one had the temerity to suggest that John McLaren receive a blue ticket in the face of storms of public disapproval." It was his boast that the parks of San Francisco were built by gardeners and not by politicians.

Up at dawn, he worked tirelessly until dark, seven days a week, fifty-two weeks a year, and he was almost as hard driving with his men. He never acknowledged failure. Nothing was too ambitious, nothing too difficult for him to undertake if it accomplished a worthwhile purpose. Peter Rock, one of his long-time assistants, says of him: "If John had given an order for a mountain to be moved, he'd have taken no excuses until it was done." But he never asked his men to do anything he would not do himself. A huge man of tremendous vitality and driving power, bluff and brusque, but secretly as tenderhearted as a child, he hid many a kindly deed, many a charitable act, under the cover of a stern face and a harsh order. By one means or another he kept his helpers on their toes, but he was almost fanatically loyal to those who had worked for him, giving the best years of their lives to the service of his Park, and so long as he could keep them near him he never let them go.

As the years crowded upon him he took on the stature of an almost legendary figure, became in his way a symbol of civic righteousness. For his services expanded as did his fame. While Golden Gate Park was the crowning glory of his life, his park interests were city wide. As ex officio member of the Park Commission he had a hand in the direction of all fifty-four of the city's parks and plazas, and so can be said to have contributed more than any other single individual to the beautification of a city renowned for its beauty. One of his conspicuous successes was his contribution to the landscaping of the Panama-Pacific Exposition. To everyone's consternation he condemned the landscaping plans already made and insisted upon their being completely revamped according to his own ideas. To carry out his scheme he proceeded to grow his own trees, planting them in tubs and boxes along the marina where, he said, they were "keeping their toes warm," but where the saplings grew at such an amazing rate that by the opening of the fair they stood thirty feet high. These, placed throughout the grounds with massings of shrubbery and flowering plants, produced an effect of breath-taking beauty and an illusion of age-old permanence. Then, the bareness of the stucco walls irked him. After some pondering he had his men lay out over three acres of ground a thousand or more wooden flats filled with earth, in which he planted cuttings of mesembryanthemum, the fast-growing ground cover of the coastal dunes. By the time the exposition was opened the plants were masses of waxy

33

bloom. Then he ordered the flats nailed to the walls in solid phalanxes, creating an illusion of walls of flowers. The startlingly original and beautiful effect was hailed by architects as the only new idea in landscape art since the days of ancient Rome. But Uncle John just smiled and called it "a simple thing"—as perhaps it was, to the "Boss Gardener."

Honors held little interest for John McLaren. Medals and degrees he shrugged aside. But carefully preserved in the Park Lodge was the George Robert White Medal presented to him by the Massachusetts Horticultural Society, the highest prize of its kind in the United States. In 1930 he was made an Associate of Honor of the Royal Horticultural Society of London, the thirty-first person to be so distinguished since the society's inception in 1804. Each year on his birthday San Francisco honored him with appropriate ceremony. Each spring, in gratitude for his generosity to them, the city's children paid him tribute.

Full of years and honors, and what must have been the contentment of a life spent in the service of his fellow men through the work that he loved best, John McLaren died on the twelfth day of January, 1943, at the patriarchal age of ninety-seven. For a day his body lay in state in the rotunda of the city hall, where thousands of San Franciscans who owed to him innumerable happy hours and the inspiration of the beauty created by his hands, passed his bier in grateful tribute. In speaking of him Mayor Rossi said: "He

34

was one of the old school of floriculturists—men and women to whom plants and flowers were living, breathing things to be cared for and nurtured as a mother would her child. . . . He is gone, but the living plants and flowers will ever remind us of a life offered in the interests of giving our people the cultural delights which these beauties of nature bring. Let us hope that, as he derived much of the spiritual from that which he created, so will we, as the days roll on, approach to some degree at least the joys which men who live in the spirit and with beauty, experience."

"It is not often given to a man," said a tribute editorial in the local press, "to live with, in, by and for his own monument. . . . John McLaren was that most fortunate man whose vocation was one with his avocation, whose path of duty lay amongst his dreams of pleasure, whose dreams were always as real as they were beautiful, who, in an unremitting success, never knew the meaning of failure, whose service was joy."

As appropriate for him as for Sir Christopher Wren would be the inscription on a tablet to the great architect in St. Paul's Cathedral, London: "If you would see his monument, look about you."

ITS PATTERN

Junipero Serra

GOLDEN GATE is the largest unit of fifty-four parks, plazas, and squares under the jurisdiction of the San Francisco Park Commission. Exclusive of the eight-block Panhandle, it is three and a half miles long by one-half mile wide, from Stanyan Street on the east to the Great Highway at the ocean beach, between Fulton Street on the north and Lincoln Way on the south. Its 993.6 acres (there are 23.4 acres in the Panhandle) are traversed by a network of paved drives based on two primary highways—Main Drive and Middle Drive, which originate at the eastern end of the Park as South Drive—a pattern of weaving roads that affords a driving distance of fifteen and three-quarter miles besides the seven and a half miles of equestrian path and the twenty-seven miles of foot trail that intersect at many points. Dozens of entrances along its four sides give access to an area that by day or by night is never closed. A single cross-town highway, with an overpass spanning the Main Drive, bisects the Park in Nineteenth Avenue boulevard which, entering at that point from Lincoln Way and describing a curve, emerges on Fulton Street at Twenty-fifth Avenue. Buses operating on this thoroughfare connect the north and south sections of the city at its western end.

39

In point of age and development the oldest part of the Park is its approximately one-fifth area at the eastern end where center most of its recreational and institutional facilities. Here are the Park Lodge, the residence and office of the superintendent; the Conservatory, the Tennis Courts and Bowling Greens, Baseball Grounds and Children's Playground, the Park Nursery, and Kezar Stadium. This section of the Park remains today virtually as it was laid out in the beginning by William Hammond Hall, and represents most of the development prior to John McLaren's regime. The establishment of the institutions in the vicinity of the Music Concourse, dating from the Midwinter Fair of 1895, came after Mr. McLaren became superintendent, and from that point westward to its boundaries credit for the Park's development belongs to him.

THE WATER SYSTEM

From the beginning the question of a water supply had, of course, been one of primary concern. The first irrigation of the Park was from water supplied by the Spring Valley Water Company at a cost of $4,800 a year for one hundred thousand gallons daily. In 1877 the Park Commission proposed some experimental well boring, but little was done toward developing a local supply until 1884, when a survey of Strawberry Valley brought a report of copious under-

40

ground streams running seaward. An ample flow of water was declared to be available from artesian wells which, pumped to a reservoir on Strawberry Hill, 412 feet high, would be sufficient to serve the entire Park by gravity. It was estimated that a pumping plant with a capacity of five hundred thousand gallons a day, at a cost of $28,000, would provide water for three cents a thousand gallons, while twice this amount could be had for two cents a thousand, an estimate which was later verified by experience. The project approved, and the contract placed with W. B. Bradbury, a successful driller of artesian wells, the work was completed in 1885, and in November of that year the Spring Valley Water Company was notified that its services would no longer be needed.

The system was later enlarged. In 1910 the plant was supplying a million and a half gallons daily at a cost of two cents a thousand. Later still, surveys of wind velocity throughout the year showed that at fifteen miles an hour sufficient power could be generated by a windmill to pump the water to the reservoir, and that the construction of a mill to pump thirty thousand gallons an hour would be justified. The first Dutch windmill was accordingly built in 1903 at a cost of $25,000. This provided an ample and never-failing supply of water at a cost of less than a cent a thousand gallons. The tower of this windmill is seventy-five feet high, its concrete foundation walls three feet thick at the base. Its blades measure 102 feet from tip to tip. In 1905 a second windmill was started at the southwest corner of the reservation from funds donated by Samuel G. Murphy, bank president and clubman of San Francisco, at a cost of $20,000. This is said to be the largest windmill in the world, slightly larger than the first, with wing blades measuring 114 feet and a pumping capacity of forty thousand gallons an hour. For twenty years the two mills pumped the Park's entire water supply. Now, however, while the mills remain as picturesque features of the Park at its western boundary, they are no longer powered by the trades, but by electric motors. All the water for the Park's score of lakes, cascades, and pools, as well as for general irrigation, is supplied by this pumping system from the Park's own subterranean streams.

THE LAKES

With such an abundance of water it follows naturally that among the most beautiful features of the Park are its many lakes—lakes large and small, lakes single and in chains; lakes for boating and lakes just to be gazed upon—lakes blanketed with water lilies, lakes banked with flowering shrubs, with clumps of calla and iris, rhododendrons and azaleas, with bamboo and weeping willow and water grasses; lakes studded with picturesque islands and spanned by rustic bridges. Into many of these, often come upon at unexpected

42

Dutch Windmill

An Island—Stow Lake

places, tumble cascading waterfalls over escarpments of natural and simulated rock and through overhangs of shrubbery and fern and nodding bloom.

A little east of the center of the Park, and in size leading the waterways that jewel it, is Stow Lake, named after W. W. Stow, a former president of the Park Commission, and for years an enthusiastic and indefatigable promoter of the lake's development into one of the principal beauty spots of the Park. The lake surrounds the rocky butte called Strawberry Hill, from the profusion of wild strawberries that once carpeted its slopes, and was specially designed for boating, with wide reaches and a long canal-like course circling the island, which is ideal for rowing and canoeing.

From the table-top summit of Strawberry Hill, reached by a pine-needle-strewn path up an easy grade, is to be viewed one of the most varied and inspiring panoramas in the world. Here a three-hundred-sixty-degree sweep to the horizon embraces within a diameter of fifty miles the Farallon Islands, offshore in the Pacific; in the immediate foreground on the west the ribbon of surf-plumed beach extending northward past the Cliff House, the Seal Rocks, Sutro Heights, and Fort Point to the Golden Gate and its poetic bridge; beyond this to the purple-velvet hills of Marin, towered by Mt. Tamalpais; and to the east the long-extended finger of San Pablo Bay pointing to Mare Island Navy Yard, flanked on the south by the

43

tawny hills of the Contra Costa country and Mount Diablo; in the eastern foreground the trans-bay cities of Oakland, Berkeley and Alameda, linked to San Francisco by the famous San Francisco-Oakland Bay Bridge across one of the world's greatest landlocked anchorages. Circling the Park on three sides, the ocean washing the other, is the city itself, its innumerable hills a checkerboard of streets, stucco structures, and plaza greens spread out as far as the eye can reach, its skyline spired with cathedral steeples and jutting skyscrapers; and finally, immediately below the hill, the great green setting of the Park, studded with lakes and pools glistening like jewels in the sunlight. Topping this incomparable outlook there was once an observatory not too poetically known as "Sweeney's Panorama," from its donor, Thomas N. Sweeney, but this was demolished by the earthquake of 1906, and has never been rebuilt. Strawberry Hill summit now accommodates the reservoirs impounding the Park's water supply. From here goes rollicking down the rocky slopes of the hill to tumble into Stow Lake the stream that is Huntington Falls, the largest waterfall in the Park, constructed at a cost of $25,000, the gift of Collis P. Huntington, of railroad fame.

Next in size to Stow is Spreckels Lake near the Fulton Street boundary at Thirty-third Avenue, also a recreational water frequented by amateur yachtsmen with their model sailboats and motor craft. Here on breezy days may be seen a dozen miniature yachts, many of them works of expert handicraft, being set skillfully a-sail by men and boy enthusiasts from vantage points along the grassy shore. Some of these small craft are radio controlled; others are geared to the aeronautics of sail, their courses controlled by their sailors on shore. Regattas are held with these play boats and the sport has developed a coterie of yachtsmen who, in a clubhouse snugged among rhododendrons near the lake, promote the interests and activities connected with their hobby.

Other sizeable lakes are Mallard, Metson, South, North, Lloyd, Alvord and Elk Glen, each with its own special interest and beauty, and each a sanctuary for the flocks of wild fowl that know so well the safety of the Park. One of the loveliest groups is the Chain of Lakes that crosses the Park diagonally toward its western end, a series of pools where skillful adaptation of the natural conditions has created a succession of waterways joined by grass-bordered inlets, islets and small isthmuses. Seven islands dotting the lakes are clothed with grasses and shrubs, while the shores are bordered with birches, willows, alders, bamboos and acacias, and studded with iris and rhododendron.

The lakes are all, of course, artificially made, their bottoms watertight through the skillful use of clay, gravel, and rock tamped down to an impervious hardness. They owe their existence and their beauty to the careful planning and sound construction of John McLaren. The lakes were for the most part named after former members of the Park Commission, and lie chiefly in the western section of the Park which it was John McLaren's dream to make a place of natural, rustic beauty.

THE MEADOWS

The Park's meadows, long and spacious, and lying well below the level of the driveways, serve many and varied uses. As picnic grounds some are provided with rustic tables and benches, and any day will find them dotted with groups busy at baskets and hampers. The largest of the meadows serves as a buffalo and deer enclosure. One of the flattest is "Big Rec," the baseball field, with its space for two diamonds and three softball courts. Still another of the large meadows accommodates the Children's Playground. One of the most charming of the meadows is Lindley, in summer a favorite spot with picnickers and sun seekers, in winter the scene of the Christmas Nativity tableau where, in a floodlighted setting beneath a magic star, the Park sheep and their costumed shepherds present the centuries-old picture of "flocks by night." Marx Meadow is another place invariably dotted with picnicking groups, and near it, on the shores of Lloyd Lake, stand the "Portals of the Past," a group of marble columns, scarred and smoke-stained but classically beautiful, all that remains of one of the city's pre-fire mansions which was donated to the Park to stand on

46

Lindley Meadow

the shores of this delightful little lake as a symbol of other days. Romantically picturesque in sunlight or moonlight, the "Portals" are a favorite haunt of lovers and all others who delight in sentimental associations and the beauty of reflections in still waters. Other meadows of the Park lend themselves to the purposes of bowling, archery, horseshoe pitching, equitation, fly casting, and other sports. Toward the northwestern end of the Park is the Old Speedway Meadow, with a length of six thousand feet, once a race track but now the site of the polo grounds and stadium where are held games and exhibitions of various kinds.

THE CONCOURSE

*I*T WAS once the "Grand Court" of a pigmy world's fair, this area that may be called the heart of the Park, the arterial focus of the life that day in and day out courses through its highways and byways. It embraces the groved amphitheater of the Music Concourse and its surrounding edifices. Here is the Park's cultural center. Grouped around three sides of a rectangle of approximately sixty acres, these buildings house collections and works of art that have been called one of the most remarkable recreational-educational features to be found in any public park in the United States. Extending the length of the northern rim of the Concourse and along the driveway that inscribes it, is the De Young Memorial Museum and Art Gallery, its Renaissance façade facing the amphitheater; across the western width is the Temple of Music; on the southern boundary are grouped the buildings of the California Academy of Sciences and the Steinhart Aquarium—all set within frames of verdure designed to give each its effective place in the landscaping; while the eastern end and portions of the driveway skirting the Concourse on the south are hedge-screened areas reserved for parking purposes.

As a Grand Court it dates back to the years immediately following the World's Columbian Exposition of 1893 at Chicago, at whose close M. H. De Young, publisher of the *San Francisco Chronicle,* who had represented California at the exposition as commissioner at large, returned to his state with an idea. This was to have certain of the exhibits shown at the Chicago fair shipped out to the Pacific coast and a midwinter fair held at San Francisco. The suggestion took hold of the city's imagination—and the thing was done. Local financiers got behind it, buildings were erected, the grounds cleared and landscaped, the sunken garden installed, and the fair was opened with pomp and ceremony early in 1895. It proved a success beyond anyone's anticipation, closing with a credit balance of $126,991 after having lifted the entire Pacific coast out of the financial doldrums incident to the panic of '93.

But it had done more than that. It had served to introduce Golden Gate Park to the world. Thousands of visitors returned to their homes that year to sing the praises of San Francisco's Park, the wonders of its construction, and the beauties of its grounds. It was the beginning of a world-wide fame.

DE YOUNG MEMORIAL MUSEUM AND ART GALLERY

The idea of establishing a museum and art gallery in San Francisco had long intrigued the imaginations of certain of its citizens but due to a lack of funds, as well as an adequate collection with which to begin, the project had failed to materialize. Now, however, the opportunity seemed providential. Two of the fair structures, the Bavarian Building and that of Fine and Decorative Arts, had been of sound construction, and these afforded a safe housing for exhibits. They were offered for sale to the Park Commission for $75,000. Besides this, certain of the displays from European and Oriental countries, shown at the fair, were also available for purchase. Among them was the famous Doré Vase; the twenty-ton bronze urn, "The Vintage," with its bacchanalian bas-reliefs, which now stands on the lawn at the end of the western wing; the bronze "Cider Press," now facing the Museum from the terrace of the Concourse; the bronze lion now to the east of the Museum; and miscellaneous works of art in painting, sculpture and antiquities, pottery from England, France, and Dresden, to the number of six thousand items, all of which now form a part of the extensive collection. With a generous cash balance on hand, the site and building all ready, and this excellent nucleus for a permanent collection installed, what, demanded forthright San Franciscans, are we waiting for? Again, at the instigation of Mr. De Young, the enterprise was pushed and the buildings taken over, the exhibits bought and placed. And in the Egyptian-styled Fine Arts Building the De Young Memorial Museum and Art Gallery

—a memorial, not to an individual, but to the California Midwinter Fair—was opened with due ceremony on March 25, 1895, after a total expenditure of $147,000.

From the first the public interest in the Museum was keen. Donations began pouring in from public-spirited citizens—offerings, alas, too often inspired by considerations more sentimental than artistic. There were, for instance, the whiffletree from the wagon Grandfather had driven across the plains, Grandmother's fruit cupboard, and Aunt Minerva's rocker that had come around the Horn with Aunt Susie's cabinet organ; there were family "portraits" in oil—dozens of them—at the hands of "artists" with more temerity than skill; and there were hundreds of souvenirs of the fabulous Comstock era—all of value chiefly to those who gave them. The Museum was rapidly becoming a trash heap. Meanwhile, Mr. De Young was buying with his own and contributed funds, works of art in the cities of the East and in Europe—paintings, sculpture, textiles, carvings. The accumulation of material grew until the two buildings were brimful and running over. It was plain that more space was needed and a better organization and direction of the material demanded.

In 1916 Mr. De Young again came forward, this time with funds for the construction of a new building, now the central section, which was begun in 1917 after plans by Louis Mullgardt, architect for the Panama-Pacific Exposition of 1915, and completed in 1919. With the formal transfer of the control to the Park Commission, Mr. De Young's only stipulations were that nothing in the building was to be loaned or removed, that the Museum was to be open to the public every day of the year, and that no admission was to be charged. In 1925 the building was enlarged by the addition of the first wing, and in 1931 by a second. Frederick H. Meyer was the architect. In 1926 the original building—from the Midwinter Fair—was condemned and destroyed. The two sphynxes now presiding over the terrace at the eastern end of the building are all that remain of the original Egyptian-styled structure.

The Museum building is of reinforced steel and concrete construction with a salmon-colored stucco exterior, its central portion surmounted by a 134-foot tower, its façade embellished by a sandstone frieze of bas-reliefs in the classic manner, and a wrought-iron cornice rail. In the semicircle over the main entrance is a symbolic sculptured group by Haig Patigian, with other sculpture details by Leo Lentelli. On the southeast corner of the building a bronze sundial, the work of Earl Cummings, commemorates the first three navigators to land on the California coast—Fortuno Ximenes, 1534; Juan Rodriguez Cabrillo, 1542; and Sir Francis Drake, 1579. Occupying the terrace before the main entrance to the building is the lily-padded Pool of Enchantment, the gift of Maria Becker, which has at its center an island of cypress-shrouded rock bearing a bronze group, the figure of an Indian boy piping to a pair of listening pumas, this also the work of Earl Cummings.

From the time of its opening the Museum and Gallery collections have steadily expanded. With the installation of a competent director, the material was segregated, some placed in storage, and the rest organized and arranged with a complete system of labeling for the guidance of the visitor. The collection embraces a great and varied array of paintings, statuary, marbles and bronzes, European and Oriental antiques and handicraft, ethnological material, ceramics, armor, furniture, textiles, jewelry and musical instruments, coins, medals, and many objects of antiquarian interest. Recent notable acquisitions in painting are "The Tribute Money" of Peter Paul Rubens, painted in 1612, which has featured many national collections of Europe and the St. John the Baptist of El Greco.

A recent rearrangement of the exhibits has installed them in eighteen central galleries surrounding the court. Three rooms contain Egyptian, Greek, and Roman art. Two rooms for medieval art adjoin a series of galleries containing Italian works of the Renaissance, the seventeenth and eighteenth centuries. Dutch, Flemish, and English works of these periods are shown together. An original eighteenth century French room, two galleries of paintings, tapestries and

De Young Museum from Fourteenth Avenue

furniture, early German porcelain, and an Empire room are in one series, followed by five rooms housing English and American furniture and furnishings. In the west wing, containing the Californiana, are four interiors illustrating the domestic settings of the first four decades after the gold rush, together with an extensive collection of costumes worn by California women of these periods. The northeast wing houses the Chinese, Japanese, Alaskan, and Indian material, with ethnological collections also from India, Tibet, Oceania, Australia, Java, and Bali. In the east wing are held the frequent temporary local and traveling exhibits featured by the Gallery, and here are located the rooms for study and for children's art classes. An exhibition room is devoted to material for the blind, installed with Braille labels, bringing to the sightless the enjoyment of sculpture and decorative arts.

The Art Gallery sponsors many one-man shows and highly important loan exhibitions. Among these have been the exhibition of Islamic Art held in 1937; Three Centuries of European and Domestic Silver, 1938; Frontiers of American Art, shown in 1939; Seven Centuries of Painting, 1939-40; French Painting Since the Revolution, shown in 1940-41; Ancient American Art, 500 B.C. to A.D. 1500, exhibited in 1942; and many others. These have drawn very large numbers of visitors in addition to the regular attendance, which is said to exceed annually that at the Metropolitan Museum in New York.

The Museum carries on a program of educational work in co-operation with the public schools of the bay area through lectures, Gallery tours, and classroom study. Lectures and Gallery tours are also held for the general public, as are art classes and special study groups for adults.

CALIFORNIA ACADEMY OF SCIENCES

The California Academy of Sciences is almost hoary with age, as such institutions go in the West, dating back almost a century to the day when San Francisco was a rough-and-tumble mining camp still burning with the gold-rush fever of '49. It had its beginnings when the state of California was less than three years old, seven years before the pony express, and while communication with the East was by steamer and by way of the Isthmus of Panama. It is rather amazing, but characteristic of California, to realize that even then there were here men of sufficient perspicacity and intellectual interest to see that in the virgin soil and waters of the Pacific coast area there was a field rich in promise for discovery in the natural sciences—to recognize it and to have the initiative and enterprise to do something about it.

It was on an evening in April of 1853 that a group of seven men gathered in an office at what was then 129 Montgomery Street to discuss the organization of a society for the promotion of science. Of these seven men, five were physicians—Doctors Andrew Randall, Henry Gibbons, Albert Kellogg, John B. Trask, and Charles Farris. One, Lewis Sloat, was the son of the then recent commander of the United States naval forces in the Pacific; and the other, Thomas J. Nevins, served as the first superintendent of schools in San Francisco. Out of the evening's discussion came the organization of a society, with a name decided upon and a constitution drawn up. Two months later the academy was incorporated and its avowed program under way toward "the investigation and development of Natural Sciences, the collection of a cabinet of specimens and a library to embrace the standard and current works on Natural History and Natural Science, together with such choice and miscellaneous literature as may be contributed by the friends and patrons of the institution." The results of that modest program are visible today in the classically housed institution in Golden Gate Park, with its public museum of natural history and its research departments in botany, herpetology, entomology, mammalogy, ornithology, ichthyology, and paleontology, each with large collections of material gathered from all parts of the world, but especially from the Pacific area; and a library of sixty-five thousand volumes.

The California Academy of Sciences came to its present location by way of its first quarters, opened in a rented building on California Street and Grant Avenue, diagonally opposite St. Mary's Church, on the later site of the old Sing Fat Bazaar of Chinatown. Thence, in the early nineties, it moved to a building erected for it through the generosity of Charles Crocker and Leland Stanford on property at Market Street between Fourth and Fifth avenues, deeded to it in 1875 by James Lick. Here, behind a façade of stores and offices, in a setting of impressive grandeur, was maintained for fifteen years what was in its day one of the finest museums in America, a center of intense scientific activity, and for many years the only such center in western America. Around a great central court, on five tiers of iron-railed balconies supported by marble pillars, was arranged, in the museum practice of the day, a bewildering assortment of objects. Here a life-size restoration of a prehistoric mammoth rubbed shoulders with the skeleton of a modern elephant, while casts of skeletons and restorations of various animals, prehistoric and otherwise, mingled with a vast array of miscellany of other sorts. But the Museum was one of the show places of the city, and with its library and active curatorial staff, it became the headquarters for much important scientific activity.

The disaster of 1906 brought almost complete destruction to a Museum and library that had been half a century in the making, and of the thousands of specimens of nearly priceless value all that was saved was what could be carted away in a spring wagon, largely through the efforts of Miss Alice Eastwood, present curator of its botany department, who lost all her own possessions in trying to salvage those of the Academy. As usual, however, San Franciscans rallied to the rescue and offered to the Academy its present site in Golden Gate Park. Here in 1916 it moved into the new buildings, modern in every way, that house its now great collections. This inventory now includes specimens of more than eight thousand mammals, fifty-seven thousand birds and several thousand birds' eggs, sixty-nine thousand reptiles and amphibians, of which the collection from the Galápagos Islands is the largest in the world, over a million insects forming the largest collection west of the Smithsonian Institution, twenty thousand specimens of fishes, a herbarium of two hundred and seventy-five thousand specimens classified and catalogued, more than a million and a half specimens of paleontology, principally from the invertebrate field, and an extensive library.

In the west wing, first-erected unit of the building, are the two large halls containing a collection of North American birds and mammals, arranged in habitat groups before skillfully made backdrops and surroundings reproducing their native settings. These were among the first realistic stages to be installed in any museum. The remainder of this wing is occupied by the library, the botanical collection, and the research rooms of several other departments. In a corridor here may be seen a cross section of a giant sequoia from Sequoia National Park, a tree that was seventeen hundred and ten years old when it fell in 1917, three hundred feet high, and had a diameter of twenty feet.

The east wing, latest addition to the Academy unit, contains, besides the administrative offices and other research departments, the impressive exhibits of Simson African Hall. Here, in habitat groups reproduced with scrupulous accuracy of detail as to their natural surroundings, and against backgrounds of actual African scenery, are shown more than a score of groups of rapidly vanishing species of African mammals. These number one water-hole group, ten large groups, one of medium size, and a dozen smaller groups, in a collection that includes specimens of the lion, hartebeest, mountain nyala, zebra, waterbuck, sable antelope, black lechwe, giraffe, gazelle, leopard, monkey, cheetah, gorilla, baboon, and other types. The hall was the inspiration and, in a special way, the personal gift of Leslie Simson, a retired civil engineer and big-game hunter of Berkeley, who, sensible of the value to posterity of a visual presentation of these disappearing species, made the collection himself, on an expedition to Africa, and provided the funds for its installation in the Academy building. They are remarkably impressive and beautiful pictorial exhibits. Much more material is on hand for assembling when more space is available, and, when completed, the exhibit will give to the Academy a collection of African Mammalia without equal in any museum in the country.

The materials making up the collections of the Academy of Sciences have been the results of scientific expeditions sent out by the Academy for exploration and research, among them sorties to the Galápagos, the Gulf of California and the various islands of the Pacific coast, and to the South Seas. These have been added to by gifts, exchanges, and purchases. Carefully studied and classified, the results of these scientific explorations have been published by the Academy in reports, occasional papers, and memos issued from time to time for distribution to members, scientific libraries, and similar institutions throughout the world. Through its research facilities, publications, and lectures, the Academy's educational activities are estimated to reach over a million and a half persons a year.

The Academy of Sciences is the only institution in the Park not maintained by the city of San Francisco. Its income is derived mainly from endowments, of which the principal one is that of James Lick, invested in business property on Market Street. Dues of members and individual gifts are other sources of revenue.

THE STEINHART AQUARIUM

An adjunct of the Academy of Sciences, and occupying the south side of the hollow square around which the buildings are arranged, is the Steinhart Aquarium, an enchanting spot of glowing color where, in settings of emerald and aquamarine, living denizens of the deep in hues of glittering gold and silver, coral and turquoise and ocher, flash and glimmer like animated jewels under artificial light.

The Aquarium is approached across a court or terrace, in the center of which is a group of three salt-water tanks accommodating a family of seals whose antics are a never-ending source of interest and delight to visitors. The building proper, of reinforced concrete in the classic style of its associated structures, is entered by way of a wide tier of steps leading to an entrance court. Centering this court is a fresh-water pool fed by a picturesque cascade over rocks hung with ornamental tropical foliage, and containing various fishes, amphibians, and reptiles. The pool is enclosed by a bronze rail whose pillars support small balanced aquaria in which multi-hued fishes flash their colors. The walls of the court are lined with other small glass aquarium tanks interspersed with plantings of interesting varieties of vines and tropical plants.

The principal exhibits of the Aquarium, however, are found further within, arranged along both sides of a corridor extending around the other three sides of the building. Here, in large display tanks of concrete, with fronts of glass an inch and a quarter thick, and illuminated by skylights and electric lamps, rare fishes from many parts of the world, but especially of the Pacific area, swim lazily among living plants typical of their native waters. The glass of the skylights is painted a pale blue tint—this for two purposes: to give a pleasant, even lighting, and to reduce the prolific growth of small aquatic plants or algae, which constitutes one of the greatest problems in keeping the water tanks clean and the water clear. The water in the tanks, which is both fresh and salt and of varying degrees of temperature, according to the needs of their inhabitants, is kept aerated and in constant circulation through jets from glass tubes, pumped through a system which also filters and freshens the water so that it may be used over and over again with but occasional additions. The water, fresh and salt, supplied from commercial sources, is stored in concrete underground reservoirs of one hundred thousand gallons capacity, where the suspended material is allowed to settle to the bottoms so that the water will be clear. The tanks are serviced by attendants from concealed passages at their rear.

This is known as the Steinhart Aquarium since it is the gift of Ignaz Steinhart, a public-spirited citizen of San Francisco, who bequeathed for the purpose the sum of $250,000, conditional upon the Aquarium being located in Golden Gate Park adjacent to the buildings of the Academy of Sciences, and maintained and supervised solely by the Academy with funds appropriated by the city. It is the only Academy building receiving such support. Accrued interest increased the original sum to $290,000, with which the building was erected and equipped in 1923.

The number of specimens kept at the Aquarium varies from year to year, but normally it is close to ten thousand, representing some five hundred different varieties. These include dazzlingly beautiful and weirdly grotesque specimens from New Zealand, Australia, the Fiji Islands, and Hawaii, as well as from tropical seas, the gifts of individuals and organizations, and the harvests of various expeditions. Previous to the war many specimens were brought from the South Seas by steamship companies, which transported them free of charge. One collection of rare and beautiful living fishes from distant Pacific waters was the result of an expedition fitted out by Templeton Crocker, who equipped his private yacht for the purpose and devoted several months to a cruise for scientific collection and research. Another fine collection was that donated by Captain G. Allen Hancock, of specimens from the south Pacific and the tropics.

The basement of the Aquarium, besides housing the mechanical equipment for heating and lighting, and the circulation of air and water, contains the Aquarium offices, a library, and research laboratory, the latter fully equipped for both chemical and biological work. Here problems relating to fish and to aquatic life in general are studied, as well as the chemistry of the waters in which they live. On the main floor is also an experimental hatchery.

The Aquarium is one of the most fascinating and popular of all exhibits in the Park, having attracted an average of some nine hundred and fifty thousand visitors a year since its beginning. It is a favorite mecca for classes from the public and private schools, for clubs and other organizations with a leaning toward scientific research. For these groups, guides are provided, as far as possible, for the purpose of extending the educational advantages. The building is already inadequate for the accommodation of its visitors—there have been as many as ten thousand in a day—and for the reference, research, and other public services which are among the wider aims of the Academy, but any enlargement of facilities must await further endowment.

THE TEMPLE OF MUSIC

The classic Temple of Music which presides impressively over the main Concourse—that "Concert Valley" of the old fair site—and from whose rostrum the Park Band presents its Sunday afternoon concerts, was the gift of Claus Spreckels, designed in collaboration with the ideas of John McLaren. Built in 1899 at a cost of $75,000, it is a stately structure of Colusa sandstone in the style of the Italian Renaissance, designed and constructed by Reid Brothers. It consists of a central section fifty-five feet wide by seventy feet high, supported on each side by Corinthian columns, the frontal arch between bearing decorative bas-reliefs. It is flanked on each side by a colonnade of sixteen Ionic columns fifty-two and a half feet high by fifteen feet in depth. This pillared area is reached by steps from the sunken amphitheater before it and the driveway skirting it. In its center is the orchestra niche, fifty-five feet wide, with seating capacity for a hundred musicians. And behind this are rooms for the musicians' assembly, and for the care and storage of instruments and music.

Facing the Temple over an area of some thirty acres extends the Music Concourse proper, the sunken-garden grove of elms, lindens, and sycamores that forms the Park's great amphitheater. Here in its dappled shade, to the tinkle of fountains, amid the perfume from its flower-bedded terraces, and bathed in the sunlight which flickers through the interlacings of its clipped bowering trees, the city's music-loving throngs gather on Sunday afternoons and on holiday occasions to listen to concerts by the Park's competent Band which, under the direction of Ralph Murray, has been performing this service for more than twenty years. It is a scene with something of the Old World flavor of charm and sociability, given a cosmopolitan air by those homogeneous groups from the city's Spanish, Italian, French, Russian, and Chinese quarters, drawn together by the love of music and friendly association. They come in large numbers on Sunday afternoons, and on special holidays the amphitheater is taxed to its twenty thousand capacity, for the music is good. The Park Band is one of the insti-

Across the Concourse: Temple of Music and De Young Museum

Entrance to Tea Garden

tutions which has a special contribution to make to the culture of the city's people. Its programs are planned with taste and discrimination, its execution is of the best, its offerings are generous.

Typical of the special programs given by the Band is this one, presented as an Easter Sunday concert:

Hallelujah Chorus from "The Messiah" - - *Handel*
Overture—"Calif of Bagdad" - - - - - *Boieldieu*
"Spring, Beautiful Spring" - - - - - - - *Lincke*
Reverie—"In a Monastery Garden" - - - *Ketelbey*
Selection from "Cavalleria Rusticana" - - *Mascagni*
"Spring Song" - - - - - - - - - *Mendelssohn*
"Easter Parade" - - - - - - - - - - *Berlin*
Good Friday Music from "Parsifal" - - - - *Wagner*
Descriptive Piece—"A Hunting Scene" - - *Bucalossi*
Fantasie—"Onward, Christian Soldiers" - - *Sullivan*

This program, commemorating the one hundredth anniversary of the birth of John McLaren, was given on December 15, 1946, and is of special interest:

National Anthem
Reminiscences of Scotland - - - - - - - *Godfrey*
Waltz, Lysistrata - - - - - - - - - - *Lincke*
Selection, "Daughter of the Regiment" - - *Donizetti*
"The Night Was Made for Love" - - - - *Kern*
Fantasy and Fugue, "Oh, Susanna" - *Foster, Cailliett*
Lullaby - - - - - - - - - - - - - *Patlain*
Mosquitoes Parade - - - - - - - - *Whitney*
Excerpts from "Coppelia" - - - - - - - *Delibes*
Melodies from "The Desert Song" - - - - *Romberg*
March, "On the Square" - - - - - - - *Panella*

69

At the northwest corner of the Concourse, across the Main Drive from the Temple of Music, is the one-time Japanese Tea Garden, now more pleasantly dubbed the Oriental Tea Garden. Here, within a five-acre tract of foliage and bloom, is the only remaining relic of the Midwinter Fair of 1895 where, less familiar then than now, this bit of garden art was one of the unique and most admired features. Into it through a two-storied *ro-mon,* or gate, of *hinoki* wood one went along narrow, winding paths, around limpid pools and lichened rockeries, over rustic bridges flanked by *bonsai,* or dwarfed conifers, some more than a century old, through a series of miniature landscapes studded here and there with lantern urns and filled with the fragrance of camellia, magnolia, wisteria, and cryptomeria blossoms. Here one came upon a two-storied *zashiki,* or typical Japanese house, with its wooden walls, sliding panels, rice-paper windows, matting floors, and inevitable tokonoma, or niche, for flower arrangements. Through other torii, or gates, one glimpsed, serene at the foot of a Shinto shrine, a great figure of the Buddha, and beyond, a circle when reflected in its stream, the rustic half-moon Wishing Bridge. Still farther along was the thatched teahouse where for three generations the women of the Hagawara family, in their gaily flowered kimonos, served tea and rice cakes to afternoon visitors. Such was the garden in other days. In recent years, if truth must be told, it had become somewhat cluttered and overgrown, losing much of that precise quality that is typically Oriental. But of late it has been completely rehabilitated. The grounds have been cleared, new plantings made, and the buildings brightened with new coats of gleaming red and white and gold paint. Tea is still served in the rustic teahouse, but now by Chinese maidens garbed in colorful *shaams*. And if the garden's transformation has borne it somewhat from the authenticity of its Japanese character into something less specific, it is still a spot of unique Oriental charm. And in the spring, when the air is sweet with the perfume of lilies and iris, and blows in swirls of peach and plum and cherry blossom, the garden is a place of enchantment in any language.

THE PARK FLORA

*I*N *Exit Laughing* Irvin Cobb wrote: "Los Angeles may be California's diamond stomacher, but San Francisco is the poppies in her hair." "Poppies"— symbol of the incorrigible love of floral adornment that inspires this coquettish city to deck herself out in the flower stalls on her business streets, in the blossoms cascading from her window ledges and balconies, in the drift of bloom along her parkway strips— "poppies," embodied in her year-round parade of floral beauty through her Golden Gate Park.

It begins in February and March with the first of the spectacular rhododendrons, the scarlet cornubia, drawn up in ranks along the driveways or standing in squads among the trees. Falconeri follows close on cornubia's heels in March, an army of descendants from a plant imported from Kew Gardens, London, but native to India, where it grows to a height of seventy or eighty feet. In April come marching along the various groups from western China, notably the fragrant Himalayan species, these largely assembled on the South Drive near the Twentieth Avenue entrance—to be followed in early May by the lovely Pink Pearl and Cynthia, especially fine groups of these being found in De Laveaga Dell. Mid-May brings a company of many hybrids, commonly called catawba, varied assemblages of which may be seen in many places, but particularly in the Shakespeare Garden. June virtually ends the rhododendron pageant with Parsons' grandiflorum and decorum. It is an inspiring show, the rhododendron parade, perhaps the Park's proudest display, since it is to the propagation of these more than two hundred species of a plant difficult of culture in many places, that the Park botanists have given most intensive thought and care. Running the gamut from the purest white through cream, pink and rose, lavender and purple, scarlet, American beauty, crimson and wine, in great clusters of gorgeous bloom, it makes of the Park in springtime a place of unbelievable beauty.

Along with the rhododendrons and azaleas (of the same family) come all the other springtime blooms— the bedded masses of daffodils, jonquils and crocuses (and in prewar times, the tulips); among the trees and shrubs the peach and quince and cherry blossoms, the pink and the white dogwood, the feather-flowered eucalyptus in hues of cream and scarlet and coral; the camellias, with their waxy rosettes of cream and pink and rose; and the flaunting blossoms of the magnolia and tulip trees.

Early summer brings the irises and the callas, grouped along the lakes and pools to nod and smile, narcissus-like, at their own reflections; and in the semishade of the glens and along the driveways, man-

76

Tree Ferns

high clumps of fuchsias with their pendant jewels of glowing color. Then, too, in masses everywhere, all the usual summer flowers—delphinium, gladiolus, and snapdragon, pansy, marguerite and Shasta daisy, and borders of pink and crimson begonia—to list them would be to catalogue every species of flower common to the Temperate Zone.

With late summer and early autumn arrive the splendid dahlias, their regimental colors held high above the ranks of surrounding green. Specially fine displays of these are to be found in the grounds about the Conservatory. Autumn also ushers in the many-hued asters, the great clumps of pastel-toned hydrangeas, the scarlet cannas and masses of salvia, but most commanding of all, the lordly chrysanthemum, in size and hue running from dainty miniature buttons to the gigantic cabbages used in football corsages. Now, too, appear the berried shrubs, with their contributions of winter color in the orange-red clusters of the Pyracanthas and the crimson beads of the Cotoneaster and bayberry; and serving as a modest foil to them, the various mauves of the many types of heather that line the driveways, blossoming, as do many of the autumn flowers, the winter through.

A catalogue of the Park's trees, plants, and shrubs, and the story of their propagation, is material for a volume in itself. When it is remembered that every growing thing in the Park's thousand acres, other than the ubiquitous weed, has been planted there, some idea is had of the extent of its flora and of the labor that has gone into its creation. Oldest, hardiest, and most numerous of the Park's trees are the cypresses, pines, and eucalypti, to which it owes it very existence. Of these, there are twenty-two different varieties of pine, eight of cypress, and more than a hundred of eucalyptus, the latter native of Australia, New Zealand, and the Orient—places, incidentally, from which plants find themselves quite at home in the California climate. The Park boasts some fine examples of the native but slow-growing redwood, planted, according to their habit, in clumps and groves. Many cedars and spruces from the cooler zones are successfully grown in the Park, of which there are three or four varieties of each. Of the deciduous trees the principal types are the elm, plane, oak, maple, linden, and ash, with the bay and acacia most numerous and often doubling as shrubs in the roles of fillers. All in all, there are some four thousand varieties of trees in the Park.

Commonest and most space-filling among the shrubs is the New Zealand tea plant, each voluminous bush a cloud of delicate white blossom in the spring and a mass of plume-like green foliage throughout the year. A happy companion to it in the delicacy of its leafage and the laciness of its yellow bloom, and always first out in the spring, is the varied acacia, with its contrasting smoky foliage, gray-green throughout the year.

Everywhere in the Park one sees the escallonia with

its shiny leaves and clusters of bell-shaped flowers in red, white, and pink, while fully as common and as generously blooming are the various species of Veronica, with their lacy panicles in shades of white, pink, lavender, wine, and purple. Running a good third among the predominant shrubs is the white-, yellow-, and blue-flowered pittosporum, another Australian native that finds the Park setting much to its liking.

Never failing to attract the eye and admiration of Park visitors are the tropical tree ferns, groups of which line the Main Drive at various points and form one of the outstanding features of De Laveaga Dell and of the lily pond now gracing an old quarry opposite the Conservatory. Startling in the size of the great fronds that fan out from a single trunklike stem to heights well above the surrounding greenery, they are picturesque incidents in the landscape wherever they are come upon.

The Strybing Arboretum and Botanical Garden

Here is what may fitly be called the "Plant Treasury" of Golden Gate Park. For into this forty-acre botanical garden have been gathered, for their protection and security, as well as their expanded propagation, more than three thousand of the choicest specimens of the plant life that is so specific a feature of the wealth of the Park; specimens that number many of the finest, rarest, and most unique of the world's botanical treasures. It is one of the Park's most recent developments, dating only from 1938, when its construction was begun with funds for the purpose bequeathed by Mrs. Helene Strybing as a memorial to her husband, Christian Strybing, a California pioneer of '49. Mrs. Strybing's will stipulated "an Arboretum and Botanical Gardens to be located in the vicinity of the Academy of Sciences, in which California flowers and plants used for medical purposes shall be included."

The tract selected for the purpose was a section of the Park across the South Drive from the Oriental Tea Garden and the Academy of Sciences, an area that hitherto had not been under special cultivation but which was as large as the entire section embraced by the Music Concourse, the De Young Museum, the Academy of Sciences and Steinhart Aquarium, and the Shakespeare Garden. The work of clearing it of over-age trees, of grading, trenching and draining, of fertilizing and installing a water supply, and of erecting protective fences and gates, was accomplished, partly with the co-operation of the Works Progress Administration, according to plans and under the personal supervision of Eric Walther, master botanist of the Park, and the Arboretum's present director. Today it is a gracious landscape of floral masses, tree groups, and shrubbery clumps, mirrored by reflecting pools, an informal pattern of fascinating exhibits threaded by winding paths, for the inspection and delight of flower lovers, amateur and scientific. It is a collection of plants grown under conditions as nearly as possible approximating those of their native settings —grown with a fourfold purpose: for their human, economic, and scientific values, and for their ornamental interest.

Arboretum visitors invariably marvel at the world-wide scope of the plant life there—at the equanimity with which specimens from The Himalayas and South Africa, from Mexico and the Mediterranean, grow side by side, accepting each other as sociably as though they had not come from opposite sides of the globe. The secret lies in three salient facts: that for the most part the plants in the Arboretum are all denizens of the warm Temperate Zone; that the all-year California climate is peculiarly friendly to their cultivation; and that their homes in the Arboretum are at spots carefully chosen for their similarity to the species' native soil. Whether they have been accustomed to sunshine or to shade, to dry ground or moist, to sheltered or to breezy quarters—all these factors have been considered in their placing. For these and other reasons the collection is arranged on geographic principles, the plants of each country being grown together in a single garden. It is a system, too, which is helpful to those who view them, adding to the stranger's interest and understanding.

Each of these geographic groups is distinguished by

81

some rare or unique variety, or by some especially notable contribution. The Mexican section, for instance, contains a fairly complete collection of Crassulaceae, largely gathered from their native soil by Mr. Walther himself. Here, also, grow successfully three specimens of the famous Mexican hand tree, the novel yellow-flowered jacobina, and the Montezuma cypress, said to survive to an age of three thousand years. The New Zealand collection, which contains the kauri, a primitive pine now almost extinct, was considerably enlarged at the close of the 1915 exposition, when the fine display shown there was turned over *in toto* to the Park. It now includes various types of the rata, all known species of hoheria, and most of the beeches. The South African group features many fine heaths, proteads and various bulbs and succulents, while the Australian garden contains several examples of the famous lilly-pilly. The exhibit from South America includes various species and hybrids of escallonia, the flowering shrub seen everywhere throughout the Park. Here, also, are many novel specimens of Puya, alstroemeria, berberis and crinodendron. In the Mediterranean group is an old specimen of madroña—*arbutus canariensis*. The section given over to plants from China, Japan, and The Himalayas is largely devoted to new and rare rhododendrons, camellias and azaleas, to the propagation and cultivation of which so much special attention has been given by Park curators. Here is the original plant of the rhododendron John

McLaren, now twenty-four years old. Created by Mr. Walther, its scarlet blooms were derived from rhododendron cornubia. And here grows the famous pink magnolia, conceded to be the finest of all magnolias, and a plant which has aroused more interest and admiration than any other growing in the Park. This particular tree was brought from England (though it comes originally from the Sikkim Hamalayas) and refused to flower until its removal to the arboretum. Then, at the age of seventeen years, it suddenly put out twenty-five buds which, for two weeks in February, expanded into flowers ten inches in diameter, some of the most spectacular blossoms ever to burst upon the local floral horizon. In this same Oriental section is a thrilling mass of color presented by a bed of Chinese primroses, the result of a crossing of two species from a locality three hundred miles from Chungking, resulting in long-stemmed blooms in an amazing range of lovely pastel shades. The California garden, near that set aside for medical plants, has been planned to secure the widest possible range of color from as large a collection of flowering shrubs, wild flowers, bulbs, and succulents native to the state as may be expected to thrive here.

An unusual feature of the Arboretum, of special interest and educational value to visitors, is Mr. Walther's "Flower-of-the-Week" custom. Each week a blooming plant in each geographic section is chosen by Mr. Walther for special notice, attention being called to it by a conspicuous label, while on bulletin boards about the grounds the same blossom is "starred," with explanatory detail.

The Arboretum has been developed to its present proportions at an expenditure of less than the income from the original bequest. Plans for further expansion include the creation and development of many more flower displays, particularly of roses, irises, and fuchsias; and, along structural lines, the erection of a building proposed as a permanent memorial to Christian and Helene Strybing which will provide a botanical library and reading room, and classrooms and laboratories for the use of Park employees, botany students, and others desiring to add to their knowledge of plants and horticulture.

Open from ten in the morning to six in the evening, the Arboretum is one of the most popular sections of the Park, thousands of visitors each month wandering along its footpaths, admiring its exhibits. Every effort is made by the Arboretum personnel to be of service to visitors, to supply them with answers to their queries, and to give general information on the cultivation of plants. Parties of ten or more may be personally conducted by guides qualified to explain the garden's distinctive features and to give all desired information concerning it.

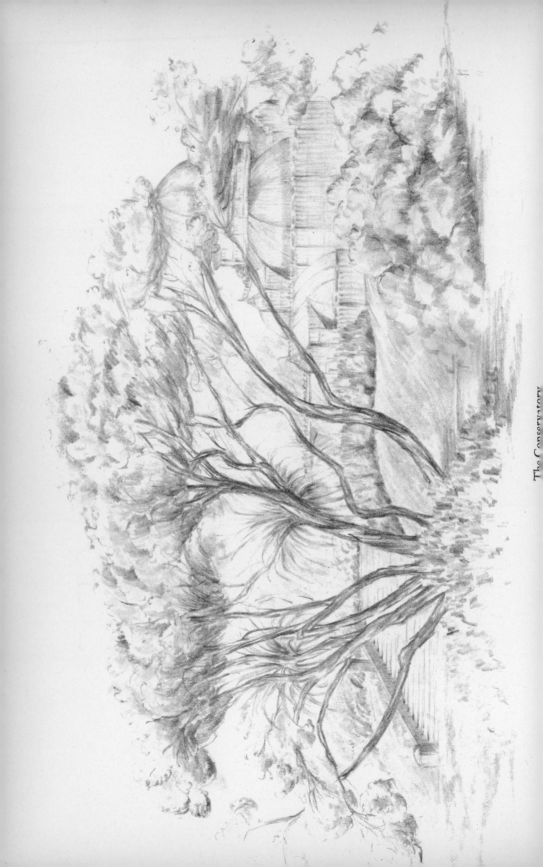

The Conservatory

This is the Park's oldest and most romantic edifice. A wood-and-glass structure, and a copy of that at Kew Gardens, London, it was originally designed to be a feature of the James Lick estate near San Jose, another of those fabulous enterprises indulged in by tycoons of that era whose rivalries in the lavishness of their establishments made of their mansions and grounds down the peninsula show places famous throughout the country. Its materials were purchased in the East by Mr. Lick and shipped around the Horn in a vessel chartered for the purpose. But its fate was to be other than that planned. Before the construction could begin, its owner was taken ill and claimed by death, leaving this mass of wood and glass on the hands of the estate's executors. Ultimately the materials were offered for sale. The advantages of a conservatory for Golden Gate Park suggested themselves to a group of public-spirited citizens of San Francisco whose personal donations provided funds sufficient for the purchase. The materials were bought and presented to the state, the gift was accepted, and the legislature appropriated the sum of $40,000 to cover the cost of erecting the structure. The group of citizens making the gift included William Alvord, A. J. Pope, William F. Whittier, James Irvine, Charles Main, Robert C. Johnson, Charles Crocker, A. L. Tubbs, J. G. Eastland, S. L. Jones, W. P. Fuller, J. G. Kittle,

M. P. Jones, J. M. McDonald, Adam Grant, William F. Babcock, R. N. Graves, Samuel Crim, Isaac E. Davis, Charles Lux, George O. Hickox, Milton S. Latham, W. W. Montague, A. P. Hotaling, Claus Spreckels, Leland Stanford, and D. A. Macdonald.

At the time of Mr. Lick's gift to the Park of the Francis Scott Key memorial, now standing near the Academy of Sciences, there had been named for him, as a testimonial, a large mound just north of the Main Drive, above what is now Conservatory Valley. This was suggested as an appropriate site for the Conservatory, and there it was erected in 1877. The building was damaged by fire in 1882, but, through the generosity of Charles Crocker, one of the original donors, it was restored the following year, and has remained as it is seen today.

A building two hundred and fifty feet long and seventy-five feet deep, the Conservatory houses a fine collection of tropical plants gathered from all parts of the world. While not as extensive a display as similar ones elsewhere, it is regarded as probably the most beautiful, both in its character and arrangement, and this, from the first, has been the principal objective of its directors. To provide a display of tropical growths of interest for their aesthetic, rather than their educational value, and to retain in the Conservatory the atmosphere of a private, rather than an institutional collection, has been the guiding principle. Arranged in harmonious masses as to texture and color, its foliage and bloom appeal first of all to the eye. Banked around lily pools, trailing from great hanging baskets, and walling the sides of the glass enclosure, the profusion of feathery green makes a charmingly contrasting background for the many varieties of towering palms grouped in centered beds. The collection boasts many rare and unusual specimens of palms, ferns, shrubs, and vines. Conspicuous among these are the tropical crotons, hibiscus, ginger, the spectacular yellow-blossomed allamanda vine, the showy bird-of-paradise flower, the strange, paperlike coral arthurium, the fragrant white stephanotis, and the splashy bougain-villaea. Outstanding among the ferns are the staghorn, of which there is an extraordinarily large specimen, and the delicate lace fern from the Fiji Islands. In the pools are various types of tropical water lilies of great size, and, framed in masses of tropical foliage plants, is the Conservatory's fine collection of hybrid orchids. Among the vines draping the entire interior are examples of the hoya, the Rangoon creeper, the Chilean bellflower, the Easter lily vine, the Dutchman's-pipe, and many others.

A unique feature of the Conservatory's year-round activities, and one that draws thousands of spectators, is the "Blossom-of-the-Month" show, when massive displays of seasonal blooms are arranged for public view. Held in the exhibition room of the west wing, these flower shows are one of the most important floral exhibitions in the Park. In January and February the public is invited to a display of the waxy cyclamen; March brings its exhibit of many-hued cinerarias; April's display is of the lady-slippered calceolaria; while May comes along with the pastel hues of the feathery-clouded schizanthus, or poor-man's-orchid. June, July, and August bring their gorgeous offerings of tuberous begonias, with September, October, and November seeking to rival them with the spectacular chrysanthemum. December, of course, celebrates with the scarlet poinsettia. Each show is an event in the Conservatory calendar and each draws its thousands of enthusiasts and flower specialists to a scene of riotously colorful bloom. It is a fact to be noted that every plant shown in the Conservatory is germinated and grown in its own Nursery. None comes from outside sources.

The personal direction of the Conservatory is in the hands of Mrs. Sydney Rich, one of the Park specialists brought up in the McLaren tradition. Mrs. Rich has been connected with the park for eighteen years, nine in the Park Nursery and nine in her present position as curator of the Conservatory.

On the slopes of the long terrace that gives approach to the Conservatory is a changing pattern of formal gardens where beds of bloom, rotating with the seasons, present contrasting masses of color throughout the year. In spring, blankets of pansies in solid and mixed colors are interspersed with beds of daffodils and narcissus, of which some thirty-five thousand bulbs are planted each year. In the late summer and fall a different color scheme is effected with such annuals as stocks, snapdragons, salvia, marigolds, dahlias and many other seasonal blooms. Here also on occasion are to be seen examples of old-fashioned flower-bed design with which the gardeners often pay tribute to such civic organizations as the Red Cross and the Community Chest with plantings reproducing their emblems. This outdoor display is not a responsibility of the Conservatory staff, but is the handiwork of Park foreman August Kusche and his gardeners, who have under their care this particular section of the Park. It is, at all times of the year, an impressive showing, attracting thousands of admiring visitors.

THE PARK NURSERY

"Mother of the Park"—so, felicitously, has been called the Park Nursery, for here has been brought to life virtually every tree and shrub and plant that grows today in mature grandeur and beauty throughout the Park. In the old Nursery, which stood where now is the Kezar Stadium, were nurtured the hundreds of thousands of seedlings which, sent from all corners of the earth, were planted to reclaim the shifting sands and, later, to make for them a cover of green. In the present Nursery of some six acres, with its two hot-houses, lath houses, and outdoor box beds, are grown from seeds, cuttings, and grafts, all the thirty to thirty-five thousand plants that each year are necessary to add to the Park flora, or to replace those that are outworn. In the Nursery are started the more than two hundred thousand pansies, and from storage here go out the thousands of bulbs that are planted in Park flower beds every year. Here are propagated the hybrids of many kinds with whose creation Park gardeners love to experiment. From the Nursery came the rhododendron John McLaren, produced by Eric Walther; here was created the escallonia Rockii, by Peter Rock; and here are grown from spores the showy tree ferns, of which there are half a dozen varieties in the Park.

In normal times the Nursery employs some twenty men in the busy months of March and September. The Nursery is under the direction of Lewis C. Allen, another of the McLaren gardeners whose connection with the Park dates back thirty-five years.

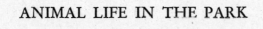

ANIMAL LIFE IN THE PARK

Buffalo Meadow

*T*IME was when the city's zoo was one of the Park's primary attractions, but of this the herds of buffalo, elk, deer, antelope, and sheep that graze on the slopes of the Park meadows are all that are now retained here—the horned and antlered species kept, perhaps, for their picturesqueness and the ease with which grazing facilities can be afforded them. All others, including the bears, elephants, kangaroos, giraffes, monkeys, lions and tigers, jaguars, hyenas, and the large aviary—all left over from the Midwinter Fair—were removed in 1928-29 to the Fleishhacker Zoo, two and a half miles down the Great Highway.

Purchased from a private herd in Montana, the buffalo group started years ago—in 1890—with three survivors from an original half-dozen, which have been increased in number by additions from Yellowstone Park, as well as through natural breeding, to the present total of some twenty animals. They share their grazing grounds with the elk and deer in a large paddock off the Main Drive near Spreckels Lake, but herd to themselves over the slopes of the wide expanse of wooded meadow. The elk, deer, goats, and sheep are less exclusive, grazing amicably and gregariously in the same enclosure, but at discreet distances from

93

the buffalo. Among them are half a dozen elk, originally the gift of Alvinza Hayward, some fifteen red and yellow deer, twenty fallow deer, and a few specimens of the Indian antelope, nilgai, albino deer, and roebuck. Some of these came originally from the collection of William Randolph Hearst, and have increased by breeding since their acquisition by the zoo. The flocks of merino sheep, so familiar a sight as they feed from meadow to meadow, are among the oldest types of animal life in the Park, having been there, as a donation, since the beginning. While the meadows afford natural grazing, the animals get daily feedings of alfalfa, hay, and bran.

The Park animals are under the supervision of the Fleishhacker Zoo, itself now under the jurisdiction of the Park Commission, Cary M. Baldwin being its director. As an adjunct to Golden Gate Park the zoo is of interest for its bird and animal population of fifteen hundred to two thousand species, cared for by a staff of twenty-four keepers. Open from ten o'clock in the morning until six at night, it is daily thronged with visitors. An average Sunday sees from fifteen to twenty thousand persons within its gates, while such occasions as the Fourth of July find more than fifty thousand parading its walks and trails.

But the horned and antlered creatures within the enclosures are by no means the major or more interesting part of the Park's animal life. Myriads of scurrying things are here, wildings cavorting among the trees, darting in and out of thickets, ducking into burrows, slithering along the grass. Plume-tailed gray squirrels, cottontail rabbits, banjo-eyed racoons, white-striped "wood pussies"—all in one degree or another may be glimpsed on occasion making the Park their casual playground—so many of them, in fact, that their number has to be kept down by judicious use of the trap and shotgun. There are rabbit and squirrel families that have lived here for generations in certain chosen areas held by virtue of squatters' rights. These are common sights. But of strange and thrilling things seen and heard now and then by late strollers or dreaming idlers there are all kinds of tales— tales of the yappings of wild foxes heard in the thickets, of the gleam of a wildcat's eye in a tree's dark foliage, of a coyote caught slinking across a road. How many of these sights are the creations of over-active imaginations is something that may be left to surmise, one man's idea being as good as another's. There is always that hair-raising tale of the Golden Gate Park wolf—a silvery ghost creature seen loping through the dusk, his long-drawn howl heard above the soughing of the pines, his reality avowed by the imprints of his padded paws in the moist earth where he has passed. That he may be nothing more fearsome than a neighborhood police dog on the prowl may be granted, but it would be a pity to spoil the delicious spine-shivering thrill that the myth affords for all who love the mysteries that go with the Park by night. And there was that tale, years back, of the banshee—a great white shape seen night after night floating among the trees and emitting wild, unearthly cries that trailed back weirdly through the shadows. This was a banshee, though, whose material body can be viewed today in the Academy of Sciences where, stuffed and mounted after having been bagged by a Park keeper, it stands a greater mystery in materiality than was ever its ghostly immateriality. For this proved to be a great white owl whose habitat is the Alaskan tundra beyond the Arctic Circle, and by what lure or guidance it had found its way south across thousands of miles of alien land to bring up in Golden Gate Park remains one of the mysteries that will never be explained.

The Park is a refuge for all sorts of fowl, wild and domestic. Well aware of their complete safety among the pools and lakes of Golden Gate Park, almost every variety of waterfowl makes this a way station on its seasonal migrations, leaving and returning year after year in comfortable assurance of the abundant feeding awaiting it at the hands of Park keepers and Park visitors. Mallard and teal, butterball and canvasback, sprig, broadbill, spoonbill, white brant, mud hen and geese of various kinds—all mingle happily with the stately black and white swans and pelicans, as well as with their own domestic kind, whose fledglings, mothered along the shores, are themselves as indifferent to their migrating cousins as to the human amphibians skimming here and there in rowboats or canoes.

Quail, protected in California to the point of nuisances, have long since grown used to men, and often in the spring coveys of fifty or more will suddenly stream out from a thicket to scurry across a road or a meadow, each fussy mother trailed by a flock of puffballs. Peacocks and pheasants strutting their stuff in plain view along the drives are occasionally seen, but these have largely retreated to thickets and protected glens where, however, they are easily found by those that know the place to look for them. The pheasants include in their number the golden, silvern, and copper varieties, and others from China, England, and Central America, embracing the piebald, ringneck, blue neck, Lady Amherst and Lady Reeves species.

In the days of the Park zoo the collection boasted a large aviary, another legacy from the Midwinter Fair, where hundreds of singing birds included the American and Japanese nightingales, goldfinches, linnets, canaries, mockingbirds and skylarks, besides the less vocal doves, lovebirds, owls, eagles, thrushes, sparrows, macaws, mandarin ducks, pigeons, chicken hawks, and guinea fowl. The aviary, however, has followed the zoo to the Fleishhacker grounds, leaving the Park to the wild native birds that in all seasons of the year keep it atwitter with the chirpings of the thousands that nest there.

Enjoyment of the wild life in the Park is more often than not a matter of seeking out a secluded spot and sitting for a motionless few minutes to wait for a bird

97

or a groundling to appear. He invariably does. And it is one of the delightful things about the Park that whatever he is, he doesn't in the least mind your intrusion!

NATURAL MEMORIALS

*I*NHERENT in the character of the Park is the fact that in so many ways it lends itself to recognition of significant events, achievements, and personalities through living and natural forms of memorial. The long life of the California redwoods, for instance, and the almost unlimited scope of the trees, shrubs, and flowers that thrive in the California climate, offer endless opportunity for the expression of sentimental tributes.

JOHN McLAREN RHODODENDRON DELL

Set apart as a memorial to John McLaren is a twenty-acre tract on the Main Drive near the Sixth Avenue entrance, known as the John McLaren Rhododendron Dell. Here is a massed planting of the rhododendron bearing his name, ultimately to be the largest single display of the flower in the Park. The tract is still in process of development.

REDWOOD MEMORIAL GROVE

At the intersection of the Main Drive and Presidio Parkway, just west of the De Young Museum, the

Redwood Memorial Grove is a group of thirty-seven of those stately trees, one for each of that number of Native Sons of the Golden West who gave their lives in the first World War. The memorial is the gift of the Native Sons and Native Daughters of the Golden West. At its entrance is a bronze statue, "The Dough-boy," the work of Earl Cummings, purchased from the Panama-Pacific Exposition of 1914-15. On a boulder at the path entrance from the Main Drive is a bronze tablet inscribed with the names of the donors.

HEROES' GROVE

North of the Main Drive, opposite the De Young Museum, is another redwood tract, this of fifteen acres, dedicated by the Gold Star Mothers of San Francisco to their sons and daughters who were victims of the first World War. The names of the heroic dead are inscribed on a granite boulder within an enclosure of the grove.

HISTORIC TREES

This is a group of thirteen trees, one for each of the original colonies, planted in 1896 by the Sequoia Chapter, Daughters of the American Revolution, commemorating the surrender of Cornwallis at York-town in 1785. Each tree has some historic association —a cedar, for instance, being one from Valley Forge; another, a tree from the grave of Thomas Jefferson, and the others have some similar historical connection.

LIBERTY TREE

At the southwest corner of the Conservatory grounds stands a handsome sequoia known as the Liberty Tree. This was planted in 1894 on the anniversary of the battle of Lexington by the Sequoia Chapter, Daughters of the American Revolution. It is said that samples of soil from various historic spots in America were brought and mingled with that in which the tree is rooted.

HOOVER TREE

About midway the length of the Park, between South Drive and Lincoln Way, stands the Hoover Redwood, another of the memorials dedicated by the Daughters of the American Revolution, this in 1935 in recognition of the work of Herbert Hoover in the conservation of the state's redwood forests.

GEORGE WASHINGTON BICENTENNIAL GROVE

On the South Drive, opposite Elk Glen Lake, at the intersection of the road from the Twenty-fifth Avenue entrance, is the George Washington Bicentennial Grove, planted in 1932 in commemoration of the two hundredth anniversary of Washington's birth.

DE LAVEAGA DELL

This is a charming ravine lying well below the level of the Middle Drive that skirts it, midway between the Steinhart Aquarium and the Tennis Courts, and approached by winding footpaths from the driveway. Shaded by interlacing oaks and threaded by a stream that feeds a lily-carpeted pool, the dell is particularly notable for its rhododendrons and fine specimens of tree ferns, one of the best displays of both in the Park. It is a tranquil spot, somewhat off the main-traveled roads, and a favorite resort with those seeking the quiet of rustic seclusion. Its wholly natural beauty has been cultivated through aid from the Joseph V. De Laveaga estate.

Shakespeare Garden of Flowers

Tucked away behind the Academy of Sciences, but approached by a footpath from South Drive, is a sizeable rectangle of velvet turf walled in by shrubbery and bordered with seasonal bloom, the Shakespeare Garden of Flowers. Here, as its name indicates, is a collection of the flowers mentioned in the poet's writings, and here in their seasons bloom marigolds and columbine and primroses, crocuses, daffodils, and bluebells—go to his plays and sonnets for the whole lovely category! Enclosing the spot are trees and shrubs of alder, apple, and ash, cedar, chestnut, laurel, and lemon, locust, orange, and pine, pomegranate, walnut, and yew, sweetbriar, rue, and thyme, boxwood and English holly. Presiding over it at one end is a glass-enclosed bronze bust of the Immortal Bard by

Gerard Jensen, a copy of the one at Stratford on Avon, with a plaque inscription explaining its origin. Off the beaten paths of the Park, the Shakespeare Garden close is a favorite haunt of mothers and nursemaids, for they are always certain here of a green-walled sanctuary for their toddling small fry. The garden was established in 1928 by the California Spring Garden and Wild Flower Association in tribute to him who knew so well such beauty as lies in "pansies, that's for thoughts," and "rosemary, that's for remembrance."

Huntington Falls

Cascading seventy-five feet from Strawberry Hill to flow into Stow Lake, Huntington Falls is the largest waterfall in the Park. It is so named for Collis P. Huntington, California magnate of railroad fame, who donated twenty-five thousand dollars toward the beautification of the Park.

Marx Meadow

One of the favorite play spots of the Park, this charming meadow bears the name of Mrs. Johannah A. Marx, of San Francisco, whose donation of five thousand dollars to the beautification of the Park is commemorated here.

OBJECTS OF HISTORIC INTEREST

AT THE summit of a knoll just east of the overpass bridge, reached by a footpath up an incline from the Main Drive, is the Prayer Book Cross, a large concrete monument presented to the city by George W. Childs, of Philadelphia, on the opening of the Midwinter Fair in 1894, and dedicated by Bishop Nichols of the Episcopal church. The cross commemorates the first use of the Book of Common Prayer of the Church of England on the American continent, and dwellers on the Atlantic coast may be surprised to learn that this took place at Drakes Bay, California, during the visit of Sir Francis Drake to the Pacific coast in 1579. It is one of the first recorded missionary prayers on our continent, a service held on the shores of Drakes Bay about St. John the Baptist's Day, June 24, 1579, by Francis Fletcher, priest of the Church of England, chaplain of Sir Francis Drake, and chronicler of the service.

THE "GJOA"

The forty-seven-ton schooner-rigged sloop in which Captain Roald Amundsen negotiated the Northwest Passage from the Atlantic to the Pacific oceans, now stands on the Great Highway north of the Beach

Chalet near the Dutch Windmill and Main Drive. The *Gjoa* sailed down from the Arctic through Bering Strait to the Pacific and south to San Francisco, anchoring off Point Bonita, in 1906. It was presented in 1909 to the city of San Francisco by Captain Amundsen on behalf of Norway, the gift being conveyed through the then Norwegian consul, Hendry Lund. It was first beached just south of the Cliff House by its Captain Kittgard, later being towed on rollers to its present site. At the celebration of the landing, the little sloop was saluted by a group of American warships offshore. They dipped their flags in tribute to the intrepid vessel and the crew that had manned it on its history-making voyage.

PIONEER LOG CABIN

On the left of the road that branches off the Main Drive toward Stow Lake stands the Pioneer Log Cabin. This replica of the early-day settler's home was built in 1911 of redwood logs floated down the river from Mendocino County. Fronted by a fifty-foot veranda it has at one end a huge stone fireplace, and is furnished with the household appurtenances of the pioneer period. It is not open to the public, being the property of the Association of Pioneer Women of California, who use it as a clubhouse. It is, however, in the center of spacious grounds which are equipped with picnic facilities available to the public. At the

Pioneer Log Cabin

edge of the grounds, near the driveway, is the statue of the "Pioneer Mother," one of the bronze pieces that attracted much attention at the Panama-Pacific Exposition of 1915.

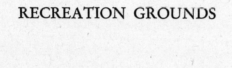

RECREATION GROUNDS

*T*HAT as a great city's recreation center Golden Gate Park should take cognizance of the varied recreational interests of its people in providing the facilities for their enjoyment was only consistent with the Park's basic purpose. And so, from football to horseshoe pitching, from polo to card playing, sports of every kind find their allotted places here.

KEZAR STADIUM

First in general popularity and in the number of spectators accommodated is the center where football contests, track meets, and pageant celebrations annually draw their hundreds of thousands of enthusiasts. This is Kezar Stadium, situated near the southeast corner of the Park on what was formerly the site of the first Park Nursery. For the purposes it serves, John McLaren had had a different dream. With A. B. Spreckels, he had made elaborate plans for the development of a great athletic field at the Golden Gate Park Stadium on the site of the old speedway at the diagonally opposite corner of the Park. But when, for various reasons of climate and transportation, this proved impracticable, the plan was abandoned in favor of property contiguous to the car lines and accessible from all parts of the city. For this, McLaren selected the present location. But here, too, it was found that more space was needed, and, accordingly, a number of adjacent city lots, owned by the Market Street Railway, were purchased and added to the Park boundary. Here, in 1923, after plans drawn by a committee of architects headed by Willis Polk, Kezar Stadium was erected, its initial endowment fund of one hundred thousand dollars, established by Mary A. Kezar, being further increased by an appropriation of two hundred thousand dollars by the board of supervisors. The bowl is a concrete oval enclosing space for a football field and an oval 440-yard track. The stadium had an initial seating capacity of twenty-two thousand, but this was enlarged in 1928 to accommodate sixty thousand spectators. The Stadium total cost was four hundred and fifty thousand dollars. Kezar was opened on May 2, 1925, with a track meet at which Paavo Nurmi, the Finnish marathon champion, was the feature attraction. In normal times, Kezar Stadium is the setting for many of the West's important football contests, track meets, ceremonials and celebrations of various kinds, with an average annual attendance of three hundred thousand persons.

GOLDEN GATE PARK STADIUM

The great oval inscribed by the old speedway in the northwest section of the Park area, where once the fol-

Carousel—Children's Playground

lowers of the sport of kings tried out the mettle of their thoroughbreds, had all the potentialities of a huge sport and athletic arena. Within the ellipse of the thirty-acre tract, whose grassy terraces could easily accommodate sixty thousand spectators, was room for six football fields, a baseball diamond, and a basketball field, besides the cinder track circling it on the inside and the horse-racing track on its outer rim. The grounds were, in fact, laid out and prepared for that purpose according to plans made by John McLaren and A. B. Spreckels. The track was built by the Golden Gate Driving Club and the San Francisco Driving Club, and construction begun on a concrete stadium. But the location proving impractical, the enterprise was finally abandoned in favor of the better facilities offered by Kezar, and the grounds were given over to their present uses as a polo field, football practice ground, and racing track. The field is circled by a three-quarter-mile trotting track sixty feet wide, where owners of horses kept at the stables near by exercise their mounts, many of them animals in training for racing events throughout the country. Circling the football area is a 220-yard cinder track and a two-thirds-mile bicycle track. The terrace bleachers, as they are today, seat twenty thousand spectators. The football field is used as a practice ground by teams from the city schools.

Next in size to the stadia is the football field, familiarly called "Big Rec"—the Big Recreation Ground. On the south side of the Park, between the South and Middle Drives and to the rear of the Academy of Sciences, one of the largest meadows of the Park has been made into a playground that accommodates two baseball diamonds and three softball courts. A grassy turf, surrounded by trees, it is a broad, level field, ideal for the purpose. Use of the field for games is by reservation.

Children's Playground

This is probably the busiest, noisiest, and happiest section of the Park, swarming as it is from morning till night with youngsters of the tenderer years making use of the play facilities that are among the finest and most extensive of any park in the United States. Occupying a meadow lying well below the level of the surrounding drives in the southeast corner of the Park area, it is a spot of complete safety and exclusiveness for the activities of the younger generation. The first children's playground established in any public park in America, it was founded in 1886, and with a fund of fifty thousand dollars donated by Senator William Sharon, was built the picturesque "Children's House" which ever since has served the indoor uses of the young habitués, providing playrooms for inclement

118

days and a tearoom catering to juvenile as well as adult appetites. Of buff sandstone in the Romanesque style of architecture, and swathed in vines and flowering shrubs, the house is the principal feature of the playground, rivaled in importance only by the splashy-hued merry-go-round near by, which is in constant gyration. In one section of the grounds is gathered the large assortment of play equipment which includes swings, slides, and vaulting poles. Near by, for small tots, is an area of sandboxes, and within a neighboring enclosure is the oval where, until recently, a pair of Shetland ponies had, for sixteen years, patiently served the equestrian enthusiasms of the very young. The ponies, however, having reached the substantial age of thirty years, were finally deemed to have earned their rest, and have lately been removed to peaceful pastures on a peninsula farm. Somewhat compensating for their loss are the creatures in a model farmyard at the center of the grounds, where a sleek, ruminative cow, tended by a crisply-jeaned dairymaid, has for associates a pair of snow-white goats, some chickens and rabbits, and a few other domestic animals, all spotlessly groomed and invariably surrounded by curious and inquisitive young observers.

It is a gay and colorful center, the Children's Playground. Breughel would have doted on it as a subject for his brush! Attendant mothers, nursemaids, and elder kinfolk sit about on benches or on grassy slopes in watchful enjoyment of the scene.

On special occasions there are celebrations that fill the grounds to overflowing with shouting, racing youngsters. On Easter morning, for instance, is the invariable Easter egg hunt, followed by some dance revue or picturesque pageant in which swarms of children have their parts; and on May Day there is the traditional festival when, train-gowned and flower-bedecked, the Queen of the May, with her half-dozen ladies in waiting, sweeps up in her carriage to be crowned by the city's mayor, while starry-eyed youngsters garbed in gay flower costumes, wind the many-streamered Maypoles to the music of the Park Band.

Miscellaneous Sport Grounds

At the eastern end of the Park, near the Children's Playground, are the Tennis Courts and the Bowling Greens, each with their own clubhouse and seats for spectators. Within the steel-net enclosure of the tennis section are some sixteen asphalt courts, the entire area protected from wind by a surrounding wall of shrubs and trees. From these courts have been graduated such tennis stars as William Johnston, the Griffin brothers, Alice Marble, Maurice McLaughlin, and William Tilden. The tennis arena was formally opened in 1924 with a program that included virtually every notable tennis champion in the country, playing before a capacity audience.

The three grassy turfs, enclosed by box hedges and

120

gay flower beds, provided the first public bowling greens in the United States. There are greens for both men and women, with space for spectators on their terraced slopes. A row of rare Torrey pines protects the greens from winds from the west.

To the rear of Golden Gate Park Stadium, in a bower of shrubs and flowers, one discovers Anglers' Lodge, from which one looks down upon the Fly Casting Pool with its trio of basins for practice in distance, accuracy, and overhead shots in the fine art of the whipping rod and singing line. The triple pool is of concrete construction, four hundred and fifty feet long by one hundred and eighty-five feet wide. The lodge is a charming, rustic cottage of redwood and field stone, with hand-hewn window frames and wrought-iron fittings, erected in 1938, with the help of W.P.A. labor, as a clubhouse for the Golden Gate Angling and Casting Club. Here fly-casting tournaments are held from October to June, the largest being the Washington's Birthday Handicap.

In the corner of the Park near the Dutch Windmill, is the green-turfed meadow of the Archery Field, while to the south of it, near Middle Lake, is the Equitation Field where the various arts and skills of horseback riding may be practiced.

Near the Willard Street entrance at the northeast corner of the Park are the Horseshoe Courts. Here, surrounded by trees and a stone wall, are sixteen courts, built in 1934 by the State Relief Administration. On the face of the natural cliffs to the east and south are giant bas-reliefs, one of a running horse, the other of a man tossing a horseshoe, the handiwork of "Vet" Anderson, a member of the Horseshoe Club.

Finally, in the vicinity of Alvord Lake, near the Haight Street entrance, is a spot where old men, sitting in the open, may be found on any pleasant day, playing checkers, chess, or card games at tables supplied for the purpose.

Croquet games may be set up anywhere in the grassy meadows of the Park.

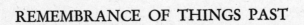
REMEMBRANCE OF THINGS PAST

*O*F THE thousands of San Franciscans who yearly find refreshment of spirit among the tranquilities of Golden Gate Park there are probably none for whom the passing scene has a more keen, if nostalgic, interest than that steadily diminishing coterie of elder citizens, the "old-timers." Any day in the Park will discover a scattering of them, frosty-haired idlers sunning themselves on benches along the drives, or ruddy-faced gardeners busy with sprinkling hose or hand rake; or even peregrinating foremen with an eye to progress in their respective areas. For as there are casual frequenters of the Park whose associations with it date back over more than half a century, there are workers who have spent their entire lives there, coming in as boys to the apprenticeship of errands and odd chores, and gradually moving up the ladder to the responsibilities of skilled gardeners. This has been true of such veterans in the Park service as the present superintendent, Julius Girod, who took his first job at the age of fourteen, grew up under the stiff McLaren tutelage in the Nursery, the grounds, and the office, and succeeded the "Old Man" as superintendent on the latter's passing. There was Robert Owen (now retired) son of the Park's first keeper, who was born there and has given his entire life to its work, and who was long one of its ablest supervisors; and Frank Slattery, one of the saltiest of the many Irishmen who worked with—and swore by—John McLaren, going in as a boy of fourteen, to remain, until his retirement recently, one of its most loyal and assiduous foremen. Lewis Allen, with a Park connection of thirty-five years, succeeded as Nursery foreman the now retired Peter Rock, himself a veteran of twenty-seven years' service. Albert Chequette, in the Park as a workman even before McLaren, was for many years one of the "Old Man's" devoted helpers. Though retired, both have managed to live near enough to the Park to be able to make frequent visits into it, with an eye to what is going on, thus keeping in watchful touch with the creation that absorbed the labors and loyalties of almost their entire lives. Old-timers all—men to whom, because of their part in its making, the Park is as dear as a child, and is venerated above all else because it is the handiwork of the great Old Man who commanded their lifelong admiration and devotion.

Of him they have many a chuckling tale to tell—of his canny watchfulness over all that went on around him; of his keen eye for everything amiss, of his bluff, blunt way of "bawling out" any man found careless in his duty. They will tell you how, as he tramped or rode about the Park, it was always with an eye for a spot that could be improved, for ways to make it something fine to look upon. They will tell you of his passion for keeping the Park natural, of his striving to have it embody the spaciousness, yet the seclusion, of the great open country; and of his struggle, by every means within his power, to shut out the impinging city by planting on the Park's borders an all but impenetrable wall of trees and shrubbery. They will tell of his contempt for mechanical contrivances, of his demand for the quality of work done by hand and by the methods of nature; of his stubborn insistence upon the use of natural materials, with horses and men to do the handling, in the shaping and bedding of his lakes and pools, his roads and paths. And they will recall the economy of planning by which he contrived to have all such work done in the winter when his men were not needed for the summer cultivation, thus giving them work throughout the year. They will tell of his stern, unrelenting demands upon the best his men had to give —and then, of some great-hearted act of kindness to one of them, performed clandestinely and, likely as not, indignantly denied. They will tell of his salty humor, his love of a joke, of the twinkle in his eye when he himself was caught in one. They will tell, in a word, of a man whose greatness of soul commanded the loyalty and devotion of every helper who ever worked with him.

Yes, reminiscing is the great outdoor sport of these old-timers, especially of the oldsters on the Park benches. Stop alongside any one of them and start a

127

conversation over some casual detail of the scene, and almost invariably he will launch off on a wave of retrospect whose wash will cast up surprising forgotten things. The whirr of a passing automobile will, likely as not, bring a nostalgic shake of the head over the changes wrought by time since the days of the horseless carriage, when, for several years, those outlandish contraptions were properly outlawed from the Park's driveways—properly, because those thoroughfares were jealously reserved for the horse-drawn vehicles that for years had made up the Sunday parades. These had been going on almost from the beginning—from as soon, in fact, as the Park's roads were passable for wheels—and had increased every year in popularity. It is pridefully recorded in an early commission report that in the year 1872-73, twenty-six thousand, six hundred and fifty carriages of one sort or another passed over the new roads of the Park to the beach! San Franciscans have ever been great for parades. These Sunday processions ran the vehicular gamut from the swanky tallyhos of the Ralstons and the liveried victorias of the Sharons and other city aristocrats, through the category of buggies, buckboards, hacks, sulkies, and surries "with the fringe on top" of the slightly less prosperous, to the dogcarts and donkey carts of the poor, to form a perambulation hardly surpassable anywhere as a democratic spectacle.

It was a parade, unhappily, not without its catastrophes—runaways and accidents, sometimes with tragic consequences as well as heroic rescues. There was that spectacular scene of daring enacted on a summer Sunday afternoon on the Main Drive when a mother and children in imminent peril behind a runaway team, were saved by a mounted officer when he roped the terrified animals with a cowboy's lariat! The tragic consequences were frequent, and in the light of modern first-aid principles it is interesting, even if futile, to speculate on the number of lives that might have been saved if there had been available in those days any conveyance other than a hack or delivery wagon, for the removal of the injured to the old receiving hospital at Grove and Larkin streets. The first real contribution to this need came with the rubber-tired ambulance donated to the city by that organization of philanthropic women, the Doctors' Daughters, which probably served in the Park, on occasion, until the police patrol wagons were equipped with spring cots, or until, in the nineties, a branch Receiving Hospital was opened in the Park itself and ambulance service installed. Maybe, after all, in spite of our present-day accident toll, there is something to be said in favor of ours over the good old days! At least our safety traffic laws, emergency first-aid services, and better knowledge of the treatment of injuries, have eliminated accidents like those of the horse-and-buggy era. We have learned a few things! Modern sanitation has given us the grace to shudder at the mere mention of the old chained drinking cups, for instance, that adorned the public fountains to the community-wide distribution of disease germs, though it is hardly a matter of pride that those on Lotta's Fountain on downtown Market Street were discarded even before the ones in Golden Gate Park.

Reference to the Park's mounted police is likely to bring forth from the anecdotists well-deserved tributes to that squad of the "city's finest" which almost from the beginning has patrolled the Park's thoroughfares with a smartness of appearance and a courtesy of manner that is a Park tradition. Those fine figures of men, erect on equally fine specimens of horseflesh, making their leisurely way along the drives with an easy carriage that speaks of both friendliness and dignity, are among the Park's proud distinctions. Nowhere has this dignity been taken with more seriousness than by the officers themselves, even if, on occasion, it may have been a bit exaggerated. It is told of an early police officer heading the Park Patrol who, sensible of the importance of his office, insisted upon decorating his uniform with the insignia of a captain and being recognized as such. On hearing of it, however, the city chief of police proved unsympathetic and, to the chagrin of the officer, ordered the insignia removed and the Park police placed under full jurisdiction of the city service, as it is today. Happily there is little occasion for the exercise of authority other than in routine patrol. Unpleasant incidents in the Park are few, and infractions of the law are rare.

Still vivid in the memories of many an old-timer is the dramatic role played by the Park at the time of the great earthquake and fire of 1906. Harrowing still are the recollected scenes of that April morning when, like the denizens of a great forest fleeing its destructive flames, the stricken city's people streamed out by the thousands, their few remaining possessions in their arms or on their backs, to the comparative safety of the city's Park. There, and in other parks of the city, for weeks and months, in tents, shacks, and other hastily thrown-up shelters, more than two hundred thousand homeless took up their abodes, living like nomads until the city could dig itself out of its rubble and begin to rebuild. No thought was then given to the beauties of the Park. Human needs came first. Sanitation, drainage, and fresh water were vital. Excavations were made, ditches and trenches dug. And everywhere in the Park was widespread destruction of the lawns, shrubbery, and trees grown over so many years with such labor and patience. Damage to the city's beauty spots went into the hundreds of thousands of dollars. Then, gradually, as streets were cleaned, refuse removed, and as the city began to build again, the refugees drifted back to their former homesites, and little by little the Park's population decreased. But for months the shacks left in their wake, many of them probably disease ridden and vermin infested, remained standing, numbers of them still occupied by persons who, claiming ownership of the property, re-

131

fused to move until the law had been called in to evict them. At last a providential fire, accidental or otherwise, disposed of the last of the shelters, but it was more than a year before the Park was cleared and restoration begun.

In less dramatic but more material and tangible ways the Park has played its significant role in the history and growth of San Francisco. For instance, through the reduction of the city's streetcar fare to five cents, another of Mayor Frank McCoppin's achievements, the Park was made more accessible to the people. This heightened public interest in it, and increased pressure upon the city authorities for its further improvement. The lowered carfare also encouraged widespread residential building in the disticts around the Park, with the result that the city's growth expanded away from its centers and thus obviated the congestion common to many cities of its size.

Wartimes, too, have given the Park an opportunity for civic service, when troops have been billeted there, necessitating its closing at night. The war-time Park has also served a peacetime use in making available considerable tracts of land to private citizens for the cultivation of victory gardens. Two large areas along the Main and South Drives were portioned off into plots where dozens of city "cliff dwellers" could be seen any day cultivating their own vegetable gardens.

Such is something of the physical role played by San Francisco's Park through three generations in the picturesque life drama of the city by the Golden Gate. What is less tangible, though to the discerning eye hardly less obvious, has been its influence upon the lives of the city's people and the development of that unique civic individuality that is San Francisco. There is no way to measure this, no way of knowing how much of San Francisco's cosmopolitanism, of her incorrigible gayety and love of pageantry, of her passion for the arts, and of her spontaneous response to beauty wherever she finds it, have come from the freedom and delight she has had in the sunshine, the color, and the fragrance, as well as in the ineffable arts of nature, viewed everywhere in her Park. There is no way of proving how much of her vitality and strength, of her indomitability in the face of disaster, of her courage for renewed and continued achievement, have been drawn from the inspiration of its towering groves, the tranquillity of its lakes, the rejuvenating serenity of its sunny meadows. But it is difficult to imagine San Francisco without its Park; the very nature of its people made that inevitable. And, as it is their own creation, so must they in turn be to a degree creatures of its subtle influences, its spiritual re-creation.

San Francisco must feel this. That must be why, when springtime comes, inevitably there arrives with it a city-wide sense of something fine impending, of some lovely, renewed experience awaiting; why, at

133

last, with the bannering on the streetcars of the glad-
some news, there sweeps over the city a long-drawn
sigh of satisfaction; why, from its every quarter, there
sets out once more the great springtime pilgrimage.
For once again new life returns; once again the rhododendrons bloom in Golden Gate Park!

Urn—Tea Garden

SUPPLEMENT

Monuments and Memorials

Erected	Name	Location	Donor	Sculptor
1894	Alvord Lake	Haight & Stanyan Sts.	Wm. Alvord	
1930	Amundsen, R.	Great Highway, No. Beach Chalet	R. Amundsen Comm.	
1917	Aquarium	Middle Dr., off Ninth Ave.	Ignaz Steinhart	
1892	Ball Player	So. side Main Dr., opp. Conservatory	Brown	Douglas Tilden, 1889
1915	Beethoven, L.	Acad. Science Drive	Beethoven Maennerchor	
1915	Benches, Marble		Dr. Florence Ward	
1908	Burns, Robt.	So. of Main Dr. at 7th Ave.	Scottish Citizens Committee	E. Cummings, 1906
1913	Cannon, Log Cabin	Stow Lake Drive	U.S.A. Ordnance	
1916	Cervantes	No. side Museum Drive, off Main Drive	E. J. Molera	Jo Mora, 1916
1887	Children's Qtrs.	So. Drive & 3rd Ave.	C. J. Cebrian	
1877	Conservatory	Main. Dr. & 3rd Ave.	Sen. Wm. Sharon	
1898	De Laveaga Dell	Middle Dr. & 4th Ave.	Citizens of S. F. Jos. V. De Laveaga Estate	
1894	De Young Museum	Museum Dr., opp. 10th Ave.	M. H. De Young	
1895	Doré Vase	End west wing, Museum	Purchase	Gustave Doré
1930	Doughboy	Memorial Grove	Purchase	E. Cummings, 1928
1919	Emmett, Robert	Acad. Science Drive So. of Aquarium	Jas. D. Phelan	Jerome Connor, 1916

Erected	Name	Location	Donor	Sculptor
1923	Fountain, Sarah W. Cooper	Children's Playground	Gold. Gate Pk. Kindergarten Assn.	
	Fountain, Child	Children's Playground		
1925	Fountain, Hearst Mem.	Steps of Sunken Garden to Aquarium	Mrs. Phoebe A. Hearst	
1914	Fountains	Music Concourse fronting Bandstand	Mrs. Charles Page	
		Center Music Concourse	Corinne Rideout	
1885	Garfield, Jas. A.	Main Dr., near Conservatory	Garfield Monument Committee	Happersberger, 1884
1923	Gate	Lincoln Way & 19th Ave.	Mrs. Christine Brown	
1908	Gate	Fulton St. & 8th Ave.	Susanna Brown	
1914	Gate, C. Clarke Mem.	Arguello Blvd.	Mrs. Crawford Clarke	E. Cummings, 1907
1904	Gate, McCauley Mem.	Haight St. Entrance	Mrs. Jennie McCauley	
1909	Gjoa—Sloop	Gt. Highway, No. Chalet	Capt. Roald Amundsen	
1901	Goethe-Schiller	S.E. of African Hall and Aquarium	German Citizens Comm.	Lauchhammer
1904	Grant, Ulysses S.	So. side Museum Dr., at Court Drive	Citizens Comm.	E. Cummings, 1906
1886	Halleck, Gen. H. W.	So. side Main Dr., near Tennis Courts	Maj.-Gen. G. W. Callum	G. Conrade
	Heroes' Grove	No. of Main Dr., opp. Museum	Gold Star Mothers of San Francisco	
	Historic Trees		D. A. R.	

Erected	Name	Location	Donor	Sculptor
	Hoover Redwood	Hoover Meadow off Lincoln Way, bet. 20th & 25th Aves.	Sequoia Chapter, D. A. R.	
1894	Huntington Falls	West side Stow Lake	C. P. Huntington	
1887	Key, Francis Scott	At Ent. to Aquarium	James Lick	Wm. Wetmore Story
1926	Kezar Stadium	So. Dr., bet. Stanyan St. and Arguello Blvd.	Mary E. Kezar	
1941	Kimball, Rose	Grounds, Pioneer Cabin		
1892	King, Starr	Main Dr. & Acad. Science	Dr. Starr King Monument Comm.	Daniel Chester, 1890
1894	Liberty Tree	West End Conservatory Grounds, near Main Dr.	Sequoia Chapter, D. A. R.	
1906	Lion, Bronze	Museum Dr., east of Museum	Shreve & Co.	R. Hinton Perry, 1898
1903	McKinley, Wm.	Baker St. Ent. to Panhandle	McKinley Monument Comm.	Aitkin
1927	McKinnon, Wm.	So. side Main Dr., bet. 6th & 7th Aves.	Father McKinnon Monument Comm.	J. McQuarrie
1921	Merry-Go-Round	Children's Playground	Herbert Fleishhacker	
1905	Murphy Windmill	So. Dr., near 49th Ave.	Samuel G. Murphy	
1922	Pershing, Gen. J. J.	Acad. of Science Drive, No. of African Hall	Dr. Morris Hertstein	Haig Patigian
	Pioneer Log Cabin	Main Dr., opp. 16th Ave.	Owners, Association of Pioneer Women of Cal.	

Erected	Name	Location	Donor	Sculptor
1917	Pool of Enchantment	Terrace, De Young Museum	Mrs. Maria Becker	E. Cummings
1909	Portals of the Past	Lloyd Lake, on Main Drive	Mrs. A. N. Towne	Clinton E. Worden, (Architect)
1894	Prayer Book Cross	No. side Main Dr, opp. 22nd Ave.	Geo. W. Childs, Phila.	
	Redwood Mem. Grove	Main Dr. & Presidio Pkway.	Native Sons & Daughters of Golden West	
	Roman Gladiator	Acad. Science Dr., opp. Museum	Society of Cal. Pioneers	
1907	Serra, Junipero	Acad. Science & Court Drives	Jas. D. Phelan	D. Tilden, 1906
	Shakespeare Bust	Shakespeare Gardens	Cal. Wildflower Assn.	L. Cardini
	Sphynxes	No. side, Museum Drive	Purchase from Midwinter Fair	
1905	Sundial	East of Museum	Colonial Dames of Am.	E. Cummings, 1907
1899	Temple of Music	Music Concourse	Claus Spreckels	
1914	Verdi, Giuseppe	So. Wing, Music Temple	Italian Citizens Comm.	Grofsoni
1932	Washington Bicentenn. Grove	So. Drive at 25th Ave.		
1933	Washington Tablet	Main Dr., bet. 4th & 6th Aves.	Sons Am. Revolution	
1894	Wine Press	So. side, Museum Drive	M. H. De Young	Thos. Shield-Clarke, 1892

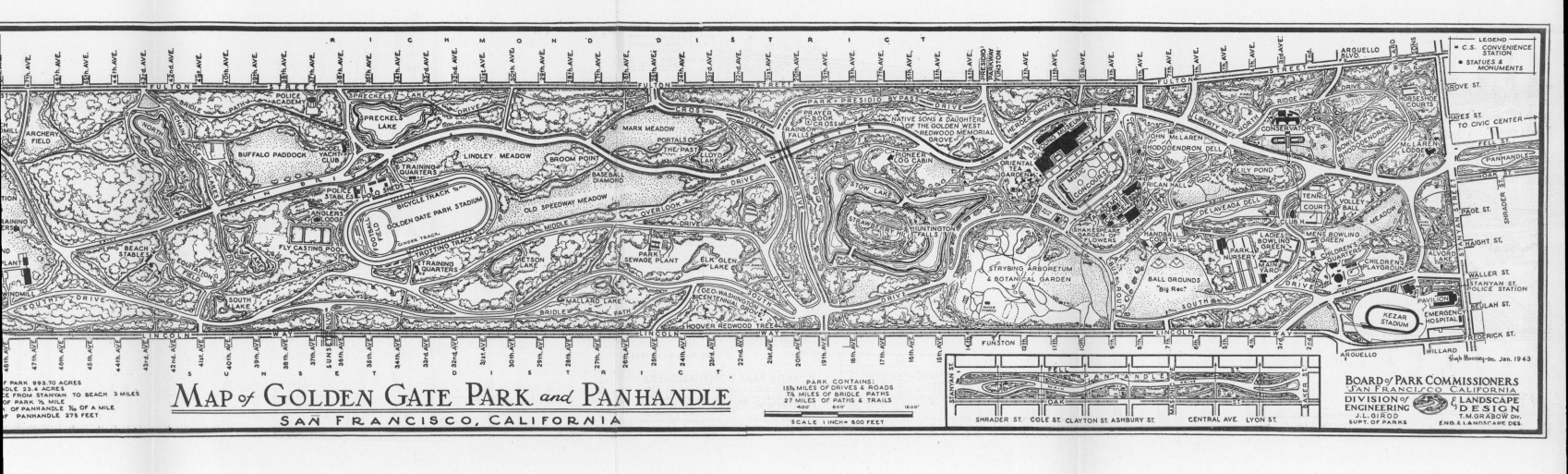

MAP of GOLDEN GATE PARK and PANHANDLE
SAN FRANCISCO, CALIFORNIA

PARK CONTAINS:
15¾ MILES OF DRIVES & ROADS
7¾ MILES OF BRIDLE PATHS
27 MILES OF PATHS & TRAILS

400'   800'   1600'

SCALE 1 INCH = 800 FEET

BOARD of PARK COMMISSIONERS
SAN FRANCISCO CALIFORNIA
DIVISION of ENGINEERING & LANDSCAPE DESIGN
J. L. GIROD SUPT. OF PARKS
T. M. GRABOW Dir. ENG. & LANDSCAPE DES.

Hugh Mooney-Da. Jan. 1943

LEGEND
● C.S. CONVENIENCE STATION
● STATUES & MONUMENTS

City and County of San Francisco
Board of Park Commissioners
Recreational Activities in
Golden Gate Park

ACTIVITY	LOCATION
Archery	Near 47th Avenue and Fulton Street
Baseball	"Big Rec"—9th Avenue & South Drive—Two Diamonds
Baseball	25th Avenue & Main Drive—One Diamond
Softball	Chalet Field—Park & Great Highway—One Diamond (NOTE: Please make reservations for above.)
Basketball	Kezar Pavilion—Scheduled Games Only
Boating	Stow Lake, near 16th Ave. & Main Drive (Not operating on Monday)

HOURLY RATES

	Week Days 2 Persons	Sat.-Sun. Holidays 2 Persons	Deposit on Boats	Extra Passengers
Row Boats Flat Bottoms	$0.75	$0.75	$0.50	$0.15
Motor Boats Electric	$1.50	$1.50	$2.00	$0.30
Excursion Boat Around Lake	Adults		.25	
	Children under 10		.15	
	Sat., Sun., & Holidays Only			
Canoes	$1.25	$1.25	$1.50	2 only
Water Bug	$1.00	$1.00	$1.00	2 only

ACTIVITY	LOCATION
Botanical Garden	Arboretum, So. Drive, opp. Tea Garden
Bowling Green	Near 3rd Ave. & South Drive
Bridle Paths	Throughout Park & Ocean Beach
Card Games	Haight & Stanyan Street Entrance

141

ACTIVITY	LOCATION
Children's Playgrounds	Golden Gate Park—Model Farm. Play Equipment.
	RIDES—All Rides Children 5c, Adults 6c.
	Donkeys
	Merry-Go-Round
	Kiddie-Kars run Saturday, Sunday and Holidays only.
	Shetland Pony Bus
Conservatory	Main Drive, near Arguello Blvd.
Cricket	Chalet Field, Park and Great Highway (For use when football season is not on)
Croquet	Courts may be set up in Park
Cycling	Auto Roads Only. Golden Gate Park Stadium. Scheduled Bicycle Races.
Fly Casting	37th Ave. & South Drive.
Football	Kezar Stadium—Scheduled Games Only
Football	Chalet Field—Park & Great Highway— Three Fields
Football	Golden Gate Park Stadium—34th Ave. & Main Drive—One Football Field

NOTE: Please make reservations for above.

Handball	"Big Rec."—9th Ave. & South Drive
Horseshoe Courts	Near Fulton & Willard Streets
Model Yacht Sailing	Spreckels Lake—36th Ave. & Main Drive
Museums	Aquarium—near 9th Ave.—Open 10 to 5
	California Academy of Sciences—near 9th Ave.—Open 10 to 5
	M. H. De Young Museum—near 9th Ave. —Open 10 to 5

142

ACTIVITY	LOCATION
Picnicking	Anywhere on lawns. Groups of 25 or more will please notify the Superintendent of Parks of intention to hold a picnic.
	Barbecue Pit and Tables at Speedway Meadow, Main Drive near 25th Avenue.
	Tables at Children's Quarters, near South Drive and Third Ave.
	Tables at Pioneer Log Cabin, Main Drive near 16th Avenue.
Polo & Trotting Races	Golden Gate Park Stadium—near 34th Ave.—Scheduled Games Only
Restaurants	Children's Quarters, near South Drive and Third Avenue. Open every day from 9:00 a.m. to 5:00 p.m.
	Tea Garden, South and Museum Drives— Open every day 10:00 to 6:00.
Refreshment Booths	Children's Quarters—Open every day from 9:00 to 5:30.
Sightseeing Bus	Waller and Stanyan Streets through Park along Main Drive.

FARES

Route 1—One Way—Adults 25c per person; Children under 12, 10c per person.

Route 2—One Way—Adults 20c per person; Children under 12, 10c per person.

Soccer	Chalet Field, Park and Great Highway— 3 Soccer Fields.
Tennis	Near 3rd Ave., between Main & South Drives. Make Reservations on Tuesday Morning for Sat., Sun., & Holidays—25 cents a Court per Hour.
Track	Kezar and Golden Gate Park Stadia— Scheduled events only.
Volley Ball	Near Tennis Courts—By Reservation

NOTE: Prices, dates and hours quoted subject to change. Telephone Office of Superintendent, SKyline 4866, for confirmation.